Nurturing Tomorrow's Leaders: a Parent's Guide to Raising a Successful Child

Barley Nicola

Published by Barley Nicola, 2024.

While every precaution has been taken in the preparation of this book, the publisher assumes no responsibility for errors or omissions, or for damages resulting from the use of the information contained herein.

NURTURING TOMORROW'S LEADERS: A PARENT'S GUIDE TO RAISING A SUCCESSFUL CHILD

First edition. April 2, 2024.

ISBN: 979-8224359264

Written by Barley Nicola.

Table of Contents

Chapter 1: Introduction

- Overview of the importance of nurturing leadership skills in children

Leadership skills are crucial for success in all areas of life, both in childhood and adulthood. Nurturing these skills in children from a young age is essential for their personal and professional development. By teaching children how to lead, we are preparing them to be effective communicators, problem solvers, and decision-makers. This not only benefits the individual child but also society as a whole.

One of the most important aspects of nurturing leadership skills in children is teaching them how to communicate effectively. Good communication is essential for successful leadership, as a leader must be able to articulate their ideas, listen to others, and resolve conflicts in a productive manner. By encouraging children to express their thoughts and feelings in a clear and respectful way, we are helping them develop the communication skills they need to become effective leaders in the future.

In addition to communication skills, leadership also requires strong problem-solving abilities. Children who are taught how to think critically and creatively about challenges they face will be better equipped to handle the complexities of leadership roles as they grow older. By encouraging children to think outside the box and come up with innovative solutions to problems, we are helping them develop the problem-solving skills they need to succeed as leaders.

Another important aspect of nurturing leadership skills in children is teaching them how to make decisions. Leaders must be able to make tough choices and take responsibility for the outcomes of those decisions. By giving children opportunities to make decisions for themselves, we are helping them develop the confidence and independence they need to be effective leaders. When children are allowed to make decisions and learn from their mistakes, they are better prepared to take on leadership roles in the future. By teaching children how to communicate effectively, problem solve, and make decisions, we are preparing them to be effective leaders in the future. This not only benefits the individual child but also society as a whole, as strong leadership skills are essential for success in all areas of life. As educators, parents, and mentors, it is our responsibility to help children develop these crucial skills so that they can reach their full potential and make a positive impact on the world.

- The role of parents in shaping a child's character and future success

The role of parents in shaping a child's character and future success is crucial and cannot be overstated. Parents are the primary influencers in a child's life, and their actions, beliefs, and values have a significant impact on the development of their child's personality and outlook on life. From the early years of a child's life, parents play a critical role in shaping their child's character by providing them with love, support, and guidance. It is during these formative years that children learn important social and emotional skills, such as empathy, resilience, and self-regulation, which are essential for success in life.

Parents also play a key role in shaping their child's future success by instilling important values and beliefs. By teaching their children the importance of hard work, perseverance, and integrity, parents set the foundation for their child's success in both their personal and professional lives. Children learn by example, and when they see their parents embodying these values, they are more likely to adopt them as well. Additionally, parents who are actively involved in their child's education and extracurricular activities can help foster a love of learning and a strong work ethic, setting their child up for success in school and beyond.

Furthermore, parents play a crucial role in shaping their child's character by providing a safe and nurturing environment for them to grow and thrive. Children who feel loved, supported, and valued by their parents are more likely to develop a positive self-image and healthy self-esteem, which are important factors in determining future success. Additionally, parents who are consistent in their discipline, provide clear boundaries, and communicate effectively with their children help instill important life skills, such as responsibility, independence, and problem-solving abilities.

In addition to providing a supportive and nurturing environment, parents also play a key role in helping their child develop important social and emotional skills. By teaching their children how to communicate effectively, resolve conflicts, and manage their emotions, parents help their child build strong relationships and navigate the complexities of social interactions. These skills are essential for success in both personal and professional relationships, and by instilling them from a young age, parents can help set their child up for success in all areas of their life. Parents have a profound influence on their child's development, and the values, beliefs, and behaviors they impart to their children can have a lasting impact on their future prospects. By providing a supportive and nurturing environment, instilling important values and beliefs, and helping their child develop important social and emotional skills, parents can help set their child up for success in all areas of their life. Ultimately, the relationship between parents and children is a partnership, and by working together to foster a positive and healthy environment, parents can help shape their child's character and future success in a meaningful way.

Chapter 2: Understanding Leadership

- Definition of leadership and its significance in personal and professional development

Leadership is a complex and multifaceted concept that has long been studied and debated in various disciplines, including psychology, sociology, and business management. While there is no one-size-fits-all definition of leadership, it is generally understood to be the ability to influence and inspire others towards a common goal or vision. Leadership is often associated with traits such as charisma, confidence, and decisiveness, but it is also about empathy, communication, and collaboration. Effective leaders are able to motivate and guide individuals and teams to achieve their full potential and contribute to the success of their organization or community.

In today's fast-paced and rapidly changing world, the significance of leadership in personal and professional development cannot be overstated. In order to thrive in the modern workplace, individuals must possess strong leadership skills that enable them to adapt to new challenges, inspire others, and drive innovation. Leadership is not just about managing people or projects; it is about setting a strategic direction, building a strong team, and fostering a positive work culture. By cultivating their leadership abilities, individuals can enhance their career prospects, earn the respect of their peers, and make a meaningful impact on their organizations and communities.

Personal development is an essential component of effective leadership, as it involves self-awareness, self-reflection, and continuous learning. In order to lead others, individuals must first understand themselves – their strengths, weaknesses, values, and goals. By developing a strong sense of self-awareness, individuals can identify areas for improvement, set realistic goals, and work towards becoming the best version of themselves. Self-reflection is also crucial for effective leadership, as it allows individuals to evaluate their actions, decisions, and behaviors, and make adjustments as needed. By taking the time to reflect on their experiences and learn from their mistakes, individuals can grow and evolve as leaders.

In addition to self-awareness and self-reflection, continuous learning is a key element of personal development and effective leadership. In today's knowledge-based economy, the pace of change is faster than ever, and individuals must be willing to adapt and evolve in order to stay ahead. By seeking out new opportunities for learning and growth, such as attending conferences, taking online courses, or reading books on leadership and management, individuals can expand their knowledge and enhance their skills. Lifelong learning is not just a personal benefit; it is also a strategic advantage in today's competitive job market, as employers are increasingly looking for candidates with a growth mindset and a willingness to learn and develop.

The significance of leadership in professional development extends beyond individual growth to impact the success of organizations and communities as a whole. Effective leaders are able to inspire and motivate their teams to achieve higher levels of performance and productivity, leading to greater innovation, collaboration, and success. By fostering a culture of leadership within their organizations, individuals can create a positive and empowering work environment where employees feel valued, motivated, and engaged. Strong leadership also plays a critical role in driving organizational change, as leaders must be able to communicate a compelling vision, inspire buy-in from stakeholders, and navigate through challenges and obstacles.

Leadership is not just about wielding power or authority; it is about being a positive influence and role model for others. True leaders are able to inspire trust, build consensus, and empower their teams to succeed. By demonstrating integrity, honesty, and ethical behavior in their actions and decisions, leaders can earn the respect and loyalty of their followers. By showing empathy, empathy, and compassion towards others, leaders can create a sense of belonging and unity that fosters collaboration and teamwork. Effective leaders also lead by example, demonstrating a strong work ethic, a commitment to excellence, and a willingness to take risks and learn from failure. By cultivating their leadership abilities, individuals can enhance their career prospects, build strong relationships, and make a positive impact on their organizations and communities. Leadership is not just about managing people or projects; it is about inspiring and empowering others towards a common goal or vision.

Through self-awareness, self-reflection, and continuous learning, individuals can develop the knowledge, skills, and behaviors needed to become effective leaders. By embodying the qualities of integrity, empathy, and resilience, leaders can create a positive work culture where employees feel valued, motivated, and engaged. Ultimately, leadership is about making a difference in the lives of others and leaving a lasting legacy that inspires future generations.

- Characteristics of effective leaders and how they can be developed in children

Leadership is a critical skill that is essential for success in both personal and professional endeavors. Effective leaders possess a unique set of characteristics that set them apart from others and enable them to inspire and motivate those around them. While some people may possess natural leadership abilities, leadership skills can also be cultivated and developed in individuals, including children. By understanding the key characteristics of effective leaders and implementing strategies to nurture these traits in children, parents, educators, and mentors can help shape the next generation of successful leaders.

One of the key characteristics of effective leaders is self-awareness. Self-aware leaders have a deep understanding of their own strengths, weaknesses, and values, which allows them to make informed decisions and act in alignment with their core beliefs. Self-awareness also enables leaders to solicit feedback from others and be open to self-improvement, leading to continuous personal growth. Parents and educators can help children develop self-awareness by encouraging them to reflect on their actions and behavior, identify their strengths and areas for improvement, and set personal goals for growth and development.

Another important characteristic of effective leaders is emotional intelligence. Emotional intelligence refers to the ability to recognize and manage one's own emotions, as well as the emotions of others. Leaders with high emotional intelligence are able to empathize with others, build strong relationships, and navigate complex social situations with ease. Children can develop emotional intelligence through social and emotional learning programs, which teach skills such as self-regulation, empathy, and effective communication. Parents and educators can also model these skills and provide opportunities for children to practice and apply them in real-world situations.

Effective leaders are also skilled communicators who are able to convey their ideas and vision in a clear and engaging manner. Communication skills are essential for building trust and inspiring others to action. Children can develop their communication skills by engaging in activities such as public speaking, debate, and storytelling. Parents and educators can also provide opportunities for children to practice active listening, articulate their thoughts and ideas, and receive constructive feedback on their communication style.

In addition to self-awareness, emotional intelligence, and communication skills, effective leaders also demonstrate strong decision-making abilities. Leaders are often faced with complex and challenging situations that require them to make tough decisions under pressure. Children can develop their decision-making skills by encouraging them to weigh the pros and cons of different options, consider the potential consequences of their choices, and seek input from others when needed. Parents and educators can also help children develop critical thinking skills by exposing them to diverse perspectives, encouraging them to think creatively, and providing guidance and support as they navigate difficult decisions.

Leadership also requires a strong sense of integrity and ethical behavior. Effective leaders are guided by a strong moral compass and are committed to doing what is right, even when faced with difficult choices. Children can develop their ethical leadership skills by learning about ethics and morality, discussing real-world examples of ethical leadership, and practicing honesty, fairness, and respect in their interactions with others. Parents and educators can also model ethical behavior and provide opportunities for children to explore their own values and beliefs, helping them develop a strong sense of integrity and moral courage. By focusing on key characteristics such as self-awareness, emotional intelligence, communication skills, decision-making abilities, and ethical behavior, parents, educators, and mentors can help children cultivate the leadership skills they need to succeed in the future. By providing opportunities for children to practice and refine these skills in a supportive and encouraging environment, we can prepare the next generation of leaders to make a positive impact in their communities and beyond.

Chapter 3: Setting a Positive Example

- The impact of parental behavior on children's leadership abilities

Parents play a crucial role in shaping their children's leadership abilities through their behavior and interactions. The impact of parental behavior on children's leadership abilities can have long-lasting effects on their personal and professional development. Research has shown that children learn by observing and modeling the behavior of their parents, making parental influence a powerful force in shaping children's behaviors and attitudes towards leadership.

One key aspect of parental behavior that influences children's leadership abilities is the level of support and encouragement parents provide. Supportive and nurturing parents can help children develop confidence, resilience, and a positive self-image, all of which are essential qualities for effective leaders. Parents who encourage their children to take on challenges, set goals, and pursue their interests help instill a sense of agency and autonomy that can translate into strong leadership skills later in life.

On the other hand, parents who are overly critical, controlling, or dismissive of their children's efforts may hinder their development of leadership abilities. Children who are constantly criticized or belittled by their parents may develop low self-esteem, fear of failure, and a lack of confidence in their own abilities. These negative beliefs and attitudes can hold children back from taking on leadership roles and pursuing their goals.

In addition to support and encouragement, the parenting style adopted by parents can also have a significant impact on children's leadership abilities. Authoritative parenting, characterized by clear rules, high expectations, and warm support, has been shown to promote the development of leadership skills in children. This parenting style fosters a sense of responsibility, independence, and self-discipline in children, which are all important qualities for effective leaders.

Conversely, authoritarian or permissive parenting styles are less conducive to developing children's leadership abilities. Authoritarian parents who enforce strict rules and punishments without explanation may inhibit children's creativity, critical thinking, and decision-making skills, all of which are important for effective leadership. Permissive parents who fail to set boundaries or provide structure may create a sense of entitlement or lack of accountability in their children, which can also hinder their development as leaders.

Furthermore, the level of involvement and engagement parents have in their children's lives can impact their leadership abilities. Parents who are actively involved in their children's education, extracurricular activities, and social interactions can provide valuable guidance, support, and opportunities for growth. By participating in their children's interests and experiences, parents can help them develop essential leadership skills such as communication, teamwork, problem-solving, and decision-making.

Conversely, parents who are disengaged, absent, or neglectful may inadvertently hinder their children's development of leadership abilities. Children who lack parental involvement may not receive the support, encouragement, or guidance they need to develop their potential as leaders. Without positive role models or mentors to emulate, children may struggle to develop the skills, confidence, and vision required for effective leadership. Supportive, nurturing, and authoritative parents can help children develop the confidence, resilience, and skills needed to become effective leaders. On the other hand, critical, controlling, or disengaged parents may hinder their children's development of leadership abilities. By understanding the impact of parental behavior on children's leadership abilities, parents can intentionally foster the growth and development of future leaders who will make positive contributions to society.

- Strategies for modeling leadership qualities and values for children

Leadership qualities and values are essential skills that can be instilled in children from a young age. Children who learn how to lead with integrity, empathy, and confidence are better equipped to navigate the complexities of the modern world and make a positive impact on their communities. As parents, educators, and mentors, it is our responsibility to model these qualities for children and provide them with opportunities to develop their own leadership skills.

One strategy for modeling leadership qualities for children is to lead by example. Children learn by observing the behavior of adults around them, so it is important for parents and educators to demonstrate the qualities they want to instill in children. This means acting with honesty, humility, and kindness in all interactions, and showing respect for others' opinions and perspectives. By demonstrating these qualities consistently, adults can provide children with a clear and compelling model of what effective leadership looks like.

Another strategy for modeling leadership qualities for children is to involve them in decision-making processes. Giving children a voice in family or classroom decisions helps them develop their own leadership skills by learning how to communicate their ideas, listen to others, and reach consensus. By involving children in decision-making, adults can help them develop their critical thinking and problem-solving skills, as well as their ability to work collaboratively with others. This empowers children to take on leadership roles in the future with confidence and competence.

In addition to modeling leadership qualities, adults can also help children develop their own values by encouraging them to reflect on their actions and the impact they have on others. By engaging children in discussions about ethics, morality, and social responsibility, adults can help children develop a strong moral compass and a sense of empathy for others. Encouraging children to consider the consequences of their actions and how they can make a positive difference in the world can inspire them to become ethical and compassionate leaders.

One effective way to model leadership values for children is through storytelling. By sharing stories of inspirational leaders who have made a difference in the world, adults can help children see the impact that leadership can have on society. Stories of leaders who have overcome adversity, shown courage in the face of challenges, and worked to create positive change can inspire children to emulate these qualities in their own lives. By exposing children to diverse stories of leadership, adults can help them develop a broader understanding of what it means to be a leader and the many different ways in which leadership can manifest.

To terminate, adults can support children in developing their leadership qualities by providing them with opportunities to practice and refine their skills. This can involve giving children responsibilities within the family or classroom, such as leading a group project, organizing a community event, or mentoring younger children. By providing children with opportunities to take on leadership roles, adults can help them build confidence, develop their communication and problem-solving skills, and learn how to inspire and motivate others. This hands-on experience is critical for helping children develop into effective and compassionate leaders who can make a positive impact on the world around them. By leading by example, involving children in decision-making, encouraging them to reflect on their actions, sharing stories of inspirational leaders, and providing them with opportunities to practice their skills, adults can help instill in children the qualities they need to become effective leaders. By nurturing these qualities from a young age, we can help children develop the confidence, empathy, and integrity they need to make a positive impact on their communities and the world.

Chapter 4: Encouraging Independence

- The importance of fostering independence in children for developing leadership skills

Fostering independence in children is crucial for their development of leadership skills. Independence nurtures autonomy and decision-making abilities, enabling children to take ownership of their actions and responsibilities. By allowing children to make choices and encouraging them to solve problems on their own, parents and educators empower them to think critically and act confidently. This independence not only builds self-esteem, but also cultivates essential leadership qualities such as initiative, resilience, and adaptability.

When children learn to navigate challenges and setbacks independently, they develop the resilience needed to thrive in leadership roles. By encouraging children to overcome obstacles on their own, parents and educators help them build a strong sense of self-efficacy and self-reliance. This self-assurance is fundamental for effective leadership, as it allows individuals to remain composed and focused even in the face of adversity. Additionally, independence instills a growth mindset in children, fostering a willingness to learn from failure and pursue continuous improvement.

Furthermore, fostering independence in children promotes adaptability, a key attribute of successful leaders. When children are given the freedom to explore different approaches and solutions, they develop the flexibility needed to navigate diverse situations and respond to changing circumstances. By encouraging children to think creatively and experiment with new ideas, parents and educators equip them with the skills to adapt to unexpected challenges and uncertainties. This adaptability is essential for leadership, as it enables individuals to innovate and drive positive change in complex environments.

Independence also plays a vital role in developing children's decision-making skills, another critical aspect of effective leadership. When children are empowered to make choices and take responsibility for their actions, they learn to evaluate options, consider consequences, and make informed decisions. This process of decision-making fosters critical thinking and problem-solving abilities, enabling children to weigh risks and benefits, and prioritize tasks effectively. By honing these skills early on, children develop the confidence and competence needed to lead others and make impactful decisions in the future.

In summary, fostering independence in children is essential for nurturing leadership skills and preparing them for success in a fast-paced and dynamic world. By encouraging autonomy, resilience, adaptability, and decision-making, parents and educators empower children to become confident and effective leaders. Through a supportive and empowering approach, children can develop the self-assurance and skills necessary to navigate challenges, inspire others, and drive positive change. By investing in the independence of children today, we can cultivate the next generation of leaders who will shape a brighter and more innovative tomorrow.

- Ways to empower children to make decisions and take initiative

Empowering children to make decisions and take initiative is a crucial aspect of their development and growth. By encouraging children to take charge of their own choices and actions, we are helping them build confidence, independence, and problem-solving skills that will serve them well throughout their lives.

One of the key ways to empower children is to provide them with opportunities to make decisions from a young age. This could be as simple as letting them choose what to wear, what to eat for breakfast, or what activities to participate in. By giving children autonomy over their choices, we are showing them that their opinions and preferences matter. This can help them develop a sense of agency and self-esteem, as they see the impact of their decisions on their own lives.

It is also important to encourage children to take initiative in various aspects of their lives. This could be in the form of helping out with household chores, taking on leadership roles in school or extracurricular activities, or pursuing their own interests and passions. By fostering a sense of responsibility and independence in children, we are helping them develop valuable skills such as time management, problem-solving, and decision-making.

It is important to provide children with guidance and support as they navigate the process of making decisions and taking initiative. This could involve offering them resources and information to help them make informed choices, or providing them with feedback and encouragement as they take on new challenges. By being there for children as they explore their own abilities and interests, we are helping them build resilience and confidence in their own capabilities.

In addition to providing children with opportunities to make decisions and take initiative, it is important to create a supportive environment that encourages and values their efforts. This could involve praising and acknowledging their achievements, no matter how small, or creating a space where they feel comfortable expressing their thoughts and feelings. By fostering a positive and nurturing environment, we are helping children develop a sense of self-worth and agency that will help them thrive in all aspects of their lives.

Ultimately, empowering children to make decisions and take initiative is an ongoing process that requires patience, support, and encouragement from parents, teachers, and caregivers. By giving children the tools and opportunities they need to explore their own abilities and interests, we are helping them become confident, independent, and resilient individuals who are capable of achieving their goals and dreams. Through guidance, support, and a nurturing environment, we can empower children to take charge of their own lives and set themselves on a path to success and fulfillment.

Chapter 5: Building Self-Confidence

- The correlation between self-confidence and effective leadership

Effective leadership is a crucial aspect of achieving success in any organization or team. A leader's ability to inspire and motivate others, make difficult decisions, and navigate challenges is essential for achieving the desired goals and objectives. One key trait that is often associated with effective leadership is self-confidence. Self-confidence is the belief in one's abilities, skills, and judgment, and it plays a critical role in a leader's ability to influence and guide others. In this essay, we will explore the correlation between self-confidence and effective leadership, and discuss how leaders can cultivate and maintain this important trait.

Self-confidence is often seen as a fundamental attribute of successful leaders. Leaders who possess high levels of self-confidence are more likely to take risks, make decisions with conviction, and inspire trust and respect from their team members. When a leader is confident in their abilities, they are more likely to effectively communicate their vision, set clear and achievable goals, and make tough decisions in the face of uncertainty. This sense of self-assurance can also help leaders to remain calm under pressure, think and act decisively, and inspire confidence in others during challenging times.

There are several ways in which self-confidence can enhance a leader's effectiveness. Firstly, self-confident leaders are more likely to take on challenging tasks and embrace new opportunities for growth and development. They are not afraid to step outside of their comfort zone and push themselves to take risks and explore new possibilities. This willingness to take on challenges can inspire others to do the same, creating a culture of innovation and growth within the organization. Additionally, self-confident leaders are more likely to assert themselves and communicate their ideas and opinions with clarity and conviction. This can help to build trust and credibility with team members, as they are more likely to follow a leader who shows confidence and belief in their own abilities.

Moreover, self-confidence can also help leaders to navigate difficult situations and make tough decisions with courage and conviction. Leaders who lack self-confidence may hesitate to make important decisions or take a stand on contentious issues, which can lead to indecisiveness and lack of direction within the organization. On the other hand, self-confident leaders are more likely to trust their instincts, make decisions based on their knowledge and experience, and take decisive action when needed. This can help to drive momentum and progress within the organization and inspire others to follow their lead.

In order to cultivate and maintain self-confidence as a leader, it is important to take a proactive approach to personal development and self-awareness. This may involve seeking feedback from others, reflecting on past experiences, and identifying areas for growth and improvement. Leaders can also benefit from setting clear goals and objectives for themselves, and working towards achieving these goals with determination and perseverance. Additionally, it is important for leaders to surround themselves with a supportive network of colleagues, mentors, and advisors who can provide encouragement, guidance, and constructive feedback to help them build and maintain their self-confidence. Leaders who possess high levels of self-confidence are more likely to inspire and motivate others, make tough decisions with courage and conviction, and navigate challenges with resilience and determination. By cultivating and maintaining self-confidence through personal development, self-awareness, and a supportive network, leaders can enhance their effectiveness and achieve their desired goals and objectives. Ultimately, self-confidence is a valuable asset that can help leaders to lead with clarity, conviction, and purpose, and inspire others to follow their lead towards success and achievement.

- Techniques for nurturing self-esteem in children and promoting a positive self-image

Children's self-esteem and self-image are incredibly important aspects of their overall development and well-being. When children have a positive self-esteem, they are more likely to have a strong sense of self-worth, confidence, and resilience. This can help them navigate the challenges of growing up, build strong relationships with others, and achieve their full potential. As parents, educators, and caregivers, it is our responsibility to nurture children's self-esteem and promote a positive self-image. In this essay, we will explore some techniques and strategies for doing just that.

One of the most important ways to nurture children's self-esteem is by providing them with unconditional love and support. Children need to feel that they are valued, accepted, and respected just for who they are, regardless of their achievements or failures. When children feel loved and supported by the important adults in their lives, they are more likely to develop a strong sense of self-worth and confidence. This can be achieved by showing affection, spending quality time together, and actively listening to children's thoughts and feelings.

Another important technique for nurturing children's self-esteem is to provide them with opportunities for success and mastery. When children are able to experience success and achieve their goals, they develop a sense of competence and confidence in their abilities. As parents and educators, we can support children in setting realistic goals, providing them with the necessary resources and guidance to achieve those goals, and celebrating their successes along the way. By encouraging children to take on challenges and persevere through setbacks, we help them develop a growth mindset and a belief in their own abilities.

It is also important to teach children how to manage their emotions and cope with stress and adversity in healthy ways. When children are able to express their emotions, problem-solve, and cope with challenges effectively, they develop a sense of resilience and self-efficacy. As adults, we can support children in developing these important skills by modeling healthy coping strategies, providing opportunities for emotional expression and reflection, and helping them build a strong support network of family and friends. By teaching children how to manage their emotions and cope with stress, we help them develop a strong sense of self-control and resilience, which are essential components of a positive self-image.

In addition to providing children with love, support, opportunities for success, and tools for coping with challenges, it is important to foster a positive self-image by promoting a sense of belonging and acceptance. Children who feel connected to their families, peers, and communities are more likely to have a positive self-image and self-esteem. As adults, we can support children in building a sense of belonging by creating a supportive and inclusive environment, encouraging positive relationships with peers, and celebrating diversity and individuality. By promoting a sense of belonging and acceptance, we help children feel valued and respected for who they are, which is essential for developing a positive self-image.

Furthermore, it is important to help children develop a healthy body image and self-acceptance. In today's society, children are bombarded with unrealistic and unattainable ideals of beauty and perfection through media, social media, and peer pressure. This can have a negative impact on children's self-esteem and self-image, leading to feelings of inadequacy, low self-worth, and negative body image. As adults, we can support children in developing a healthy body image and self-acceptance by promoting positive body image messages, challenging harmful societal norms and stereotypes, and encouraging children to appreciate and care for their bodies in a healthy way. By promoting a healthy body image and self-acceptance, we help children develop a strong sense of self-worth and confidence, regardless of their appearance or abilities. As parents, educators, and caregivers, we have the power to shape children's self-esteem and self-image in positive and meaningful ways. By providing children with the tools and resources they need to develop a strong sense of self-worth, confidence, and resilience, we help them navigate the challenges of growing up and achieve their full potential. Let us commit to supporting children in building a positive self-image and self-esteem, so that they can thrive and flourish in all areas of their lives.

Chapter 6: Developing Communication Skills

- The role of communication in leadership and building relationships

Communication is an essential component of effective leadership and plays a crucial role in building and maintaining relationships within an organization. A leader's ability to communicate effectively can greatly impact their success in guiding and inspiring their team towards achieving common goals. Through clear and transparent communication, leaders can establish trust, inspire confidence, and foster a positive working environment where individuals feel valued and motivated to perform at their best.

One of the key functions of communication in leadership is the ability to convey goals, expectations, and objectives to team members in a clear and concise manner. Effective leaders are able to articulate a compelling vision for the future and create a shared sense of purpose among team members. By communicating a clear direction and setting achievable goals, leaders can motivate and inspire their team to work towards a common objective. Additionally, clear communication ensures that team members understand their roles and responsibilities, reducing confusion and fostering accountability within the organization.

In addition to setting goals and expectations, effective communication is also crucial for providing feedback and performance evaluations to team members. By establishing open lines of communication, leaders can provide constructive feedback in a timely manner, allowing individuals to learn and grow from their mistakes. Feedback should be specific, objective, and focused on behaviors rather than personal attributes, to encourage continuous improvement and development. Additionally, leaders should create a supportive environment where team members feel comfortable seeking feedback and asking for help when needed.

Furthermore, communication is essential for fostering collaboration and teamwork within an organization. Effective leaders understand the importance of creating a culture of open communication where ideas and opinions are valued and respected. By encouraging team members to share their thoughts and perspectives, leaders can leverage the diverse skills and experiences of their team to drive innovation and problem-solving. Effective communication also helps to build trust and mutual respect among team members, creating a cohesive and united work environment where individuals are motivated to support one another and work towards common goals.

Moreover, communication plays a crucial role in building and maintaining relationships with stakeholders, including employees, customers, suppliers, and other external partners. Through effective communication, leaders can establish strong relationships based on trust, transparency, and mutual respect. By keeping stakeholders informed and engaged through regular updates and feedback, leaders can build credibility and demonstrate their commitment to open and honest communication. Strong relationships with stakeholders can also help leaders navigate challenges and overcome obstacles, by leveraging the support and expertise of external partners when needed. Effective communication fosters trust, transparency, and collaboration, enabling leaders to inspire and motivate their team towards achieving common goals. By setting clear expectations, providing constructive feedback, fostering teamwork, and building strong relationships with stakeholders, leaders can create a culture of excellence and drive organizational success. It is essential for leaders to continuously enhance their communication skills and adapt their communication style to meet the needs of their team and stakeholders, in order to lead with integrity and inspire others to reach their full potential.

- Tips for helping children improve their verbal and nonverbal communication skills

Communication skills are a vital component of a child's development and play a crucial role in their overall success in life. Verbal and nonverbal communication skills are essential for expressing thoughts, feelings, and needs effectively. As parents, teachers, and caregivers, it is important to help children develop these skills from a young age. By providing them with opportunities to practice and improve their communication skills, we can help them become more confident, articulate, and socially adept individuals.

One of the most effective ways to help children improve their verbal communication skills is to engage them in meaningful conversations. Encourage them to express their thoughts and feelings openly and provide them with a safe and supportive environment in which to do so. By actively listening to what they have to say and responding thoughtfully, you can help them develop their vocabulary, articulation, and reasoning skills. Encourage them to ask questions, share stories, and engage in debates or discussions on various topics. This will not only improve their verbal communication skills but also enhance their critical thinking and problem-solving abilities.

In addition to verbal communication, nonverbal communication skills are equally important for children to master. Nonverbal cues such as facial expressions, body language, and gestures play a significant role in conveying emotions, intentions, and attitudes. Encourage children to pay attention to their own nonverbal cues as well as those of others. Teach them how to interpret and respond to nonverbal signals effectively, as this will help them navigate social interactions more confidently and empathetically. Role-playing activities, games, and exercises that focus on nonverbal communication can be particularly helpful in improving these skills.

Another effective strategy for helping children improve their communication skills is to provide them with opportunities for public speaking and presentation. Encourage them to participate in school plays, debates, or other public speaking events where they can practice speaking in front of an audience. This will help them overcome shyness, build confidence, and improve their articulation and delivery skills. Additionally, encourage them to practice giving presentations or speeches at home or in front of family and friends. Offer constructive feedback and praise their efforts to boost their self-esteem and motivation to improve.

It is also important to teach children the importance of active listening in effective communication. Encourage them to pay attention to what others are saying, ask clarifying questions, and respond appropriately. Model good listening skills by maintaining eye contact, nodding in agreement, and showing empathy and understanding. These skills will not only help children engage more effectively in conversations but also foster stronger relationships with their peers and adults. Encourage them to practice active listening in various social settings and provide feedback on their listening skills to help them improve over time.

In today's digital age, it is crucial to teach children the importance of digital communication skills as well. With the proliferation of social media, messaging apps, and online communication platforms, children must learn how to communicate effectively and responsibly in a digital environment. Teach them about online etiquette, privacy, and safety, and help them understand the potential consequences of their digital interactions. Encourage them to practice writing clear and concise messages, emails, and social media posts, and to be mindful of their tone and language. By providing guidance and supervision in their digital communication activities, you can help children develop the skills they need to navigate the digital world successfully. By engaging them in meaningful conversations, encouraging public speaking and presentation, teaching active listening, and emphasizing digital communication skills, we can help children become more confident, articulate, and empathetic communicators. As parents, teachers, and caregivers, it is our responsibility to provide children with the support and guidance they need to develop these essential skills. By investing time and effort in helping children improve their communication skills, we are setting them up for success in all areas of their lives.

Chapter 7: Teaching Problem-Solving Skills

- The significance of problem-solving abilities in leadership

Problem-solving abilities are a crucial component of effective leadership. Leaders are faced with a myriad of challenges on a daily basis, ranging from complex business decisions to interpersonal conflicts within their teams. In order to navigate these challenges successfully, leaders must possess strong problem-solving skills. These skills enable leaders to analyze situations, identify potential solutions, and make informed decisions that will lead to positive outcomes for their organization.

One of the key benefits of having strong problem-solving abilities as a leader is the ability to navigate uncertainty and ambiguity. In today's fast-paced and ever-changing business environment, leaders are constantly faced with new and unexpected challenges. By being able to approach these challenges with a problem-solving mindset, leaders can effectively manage uncertainty and make informed decisions in the face of ambiguity. This can lead to a more resilient and adaptive organization that is able to thrive in the face of uncertainty.

Additionally, problem-solving abilities are essential for fostering innovation within an organization. Leaders who are skilled in problem-solving are able to identify opportunities for improvement and innovation, and can implement creative solutions to drive positive change. By encouraging a culture of innovation and continuous improvement, leaders can help their organization stay ahead of the competition and adapt to changing market conditions. Problem-solving abilities are therefore crucial for driving innovation and growth within an organization.

Furthermore, strong problem-solving skills can also enhance a leader's ability to communicate effectively with their team. When faced with a challenging situation, leaders must be able to clearly articulate the problem, discuss potential solutions, and engage their team in finding a resolution. By demonstrating strong problem-solving abilities, leaders can inspire confidence in their team and foster collaboration and creativity. This can lead to greater teamwork, improved morale, and ultimately, better performance.

In addition to enhancing communication and fostering innovation, problem-solving abilities are also essential for making sound and strategic decisions as a leader. Leaders are often faced with complex and high-stakes decisions that can have a significant impact on the organization. By having strong problem-solving skills, leaders can weigh the pros and cons of different options, anticipate potential challenges, and make well-informed decisions that are in the best interest of the organization. This ability to make strategic decisions based on a thoughtful analysis of the facts is a hallmark of effective leadership. Leaders who possess strong problem-solving skills are better equipped to navigate uncertainty, foster innovation, communicate effectively, and make strategic decisions that lead to positive outcomes for their organization. By developing and honing their problem-solving abilities, leaders can enhance their effectiveness and drive success within their organization. Ultimately, the ability to effectively solve problems is a key differentiator between good leaders and great leaders. Investing in the development of problem-solving skills is therefore essential for aspiring leaders who seek to make a lasting impact in their organizations.

- Strategies for guiding children to think critically and creatively to solve challenges

Critical thinking and creativity are essential skills for children to develop in order to navigate the complexities of the modern world. These skills enable them to analyze information, problem solve, and think outside the box to find innovative solutions to challenges they may face. In this essay, we will explore strategies for guiding children to think critically and creatively through various activities and approaches.

One effective strategy for fostering critical thinking and creativity in children is through encouraging them to ask questions and explore different perspectives. By prompting children to think about why things are the way they are and how they could be different, they are able to develop a more nuanced understanding of the world around them. This can be achieved through activities such as discussions, debates, and role-playing scenarios where children are encouraged to consider multiple viewpoints and think critically about the implications of different decisions.

Another important aspect of developing critical thinking and creativity in children is providing them with opportunities to engage in hands-on, experiential learning. This can include activities such as science experiments, art projects, and group problem-solving tasks that require children to think creatively and apply their knowledge in practical ways. By allowing children to explore and experiment with different ideas and materials, they are able to develop their curiosity, imagination, and problem-solving skills in a meaningful and engaging way.

Furthermore, fostering a growth mindset in children is crucial for promoting critical thinking and creativity. A growth mindset is the belief that abilities can be developed through effort and practice, rather than being fixed traits. By encouraging children to embrace challenges, persevere through setbacks, and learn from their mistakes, they are able to cultivate a more positive attitude towards learning and problem solving. This can be achieved through providing constructive feedback, setting achievable goals, and celebrating progress and achievements along the way.

In addition to these strategies, it is important for educators and parents to create an environment that supports and nurtures children's critical thinking and creativity. This can involve providing access to a variety of resources, such as books, games, and technology, that stimulate children's curiosity and imagination. It can also involve fostering a sense of collaboration and teamwork, where children are encouraged to work together to solve problems and share their ideas with one another. By encouraging children to ask questions, engage in hands-on learning, adopt a growth mindset, and create a supportive environment, we can help them develop the skills they need to navigate the challenges of the 21st century with confidence and creativity.

Chapter 8: Encouraging Collaboration

- The value of teamwork and collaboration in leadership

Teamwork and collaboration are essential components of effective leadership in any organization. They play a crucial role in achieving organizational goals and objectives by harnessing the collective skills, knowledge, and experience of team members. Collaboration allows different perspectives to come together, leading to innovative solutions and better decision-making processes. When team members work together towards a common goal, the result is often greater than the sum of individual efforts.

One of the key benefits of teamwork and collaboration in leadership is the ability to leverage the diverse skills and strengths of team members. Every individual brings a unique set of experiences, expertise, and perspectives to the table. By working together, team members can complement each other's strengths and compensate for weaknesses, leading to a more well-rounded and effective team. This diversity of skills and perspectives can lead to creative problem-solving and new ideas that may not have been possible with a singular approach.

Furthermore, teamwork and collaboration promote a sense of ownership and accountability among team members. When individuals work together towards a common goal, they become more invested in the success of the team and are more likely to take responsibility for their actions. This shared sense of ownership fosters a culture of trust and mutual respect, leading to improved communication and a greater willingness to collaborate on future projects. As a result, team members are more likely to hold themselves and each other accountable for meeting deadlines, achieving objectives, and upholding the values of the organization.

In addition, teamwork and collaboration can enhance the overall performance and productivity of a team. When team members work together and support each other, they can achieve more in less time and with fewer resources. By leveraging each other's strengths and skills, team members can streamline processes, eliminate redundancies, and make more effective use of time and resources. This increased efficiency can lead to higher levels of productivity, better outcomes, and ultimately, greater success for the team and the organization as a whole.

Moreover, teamwork and collaboration can also lead to increased job satisfaction and employee engagement. When team members feel valued, respected, and supported by their colleagues, they are more likely to be motivated and engaged in their work. A positive and collaborative work environment can foster a sense of camaraderie and teamwork, leading to higher levels of job satisfaction and morale. This, in turn, can reduce turnover rates, improve employee retention, and enhance workplace culture. When employees feel connected to their team and the organization, they are more likely to be committed to its success and willing to go above and beyond to achieve its goals. By harnessing the diverse skills and perspectives of team members, promoting a sense of ownership and accountability, enhancing performance and productivity, and fostering job satisfaction and engagement, teamwork and collaboration can lead to better outcomes and greater success for the team and the organization. As a leader, it is important to cultivate a culture of teamwork and collaboration, where individuals are encouraged to work together towards a common goal, support each other, and hold themselves accountable for their actions. By embracing the value of teamwork and collaboration, leaders can unlock the full potential of their team and drive innovation, growth, and success.

- Methods for promoting cooperation and effective team dynamics in children

Cooperation and effective team dynamics are critical components of children's social and emotional development. By learning how to work together in a group setting, children can develop important skills such as communication, problem-solving, and conflict resolution. Additionally, cooperation and team dynamics can help children build positive relationships with their peers and develop a sense of empathy and understanding towards others. There are various methods that educators and caregivers can utilize to promote cooperation and effective team dynamics in children, which can enhance their overall development and prepare them for success in their future academic and professional endeavors.

One effective method for promoting cooperation and effective team dynamics in children is through team-building activities and games. These activities are designed to foster collaboration, communication, and problem-solving skills among children. By engaging in team-building activities, children learn how to work together towards a common goal, develop strategies to overcome challenges, and build trust and respect for their peers. These activities can range from simple icebreaker games to more complex problem-solving challenges that require teamwork and cooperation. Team-building activities can be incorporated into daily routines at school or during extracurricular activities to help children develop the necessary skills for successful collaboration and teamwork.

Another method for promoting cooperation and effective team dynamics in children is through the use of collaborative learning strategies. Collaborative learning involves students working together in small groups to complete tasks, solve problems, or create projects. This method encourages children to share ideas, take on different roles within the group, and support each other in achieving common goals. By engaging in collaborative learning activities, children learn how to communicate effectively, listen to others' viewpoints, and compromise when necessary. Collaborative learning can be particularly beneficial for children who may struggle with social skills or working in group settings, as it provides a structured environment for them to practice and develop these important skills.

In addition to team-building activities and collaborative learning strategies, educators and caregivers can promote cooperation and effective team dynamics in children through positive reinforcement and encouragement. Praise and recognition for cooperation and teamwork can help children understand the value of working together and motivate them to continue to collaborate with their peers. By acknowledging and celebrating instances of cooperation and effective team dynamics, children are more likely to engage in these behaviors in the future. Positive reinforcement can come in the form of verbal praise, stickers or rewards, or special privileges for groups that demonstrate strong teamwork skills. By consistently reinforcing and encouraging cooperation, educators and caregivers can help children understand the importance of working together and build a positive foundation for future collaborations.

Furthermore, it is essential for educators and caregivers to model cooperation and effective team dynamics in their interactions with children. Children learn by example, so it is important for adults to demonstrate the values and behaviors they hope to instill in children. By modeling cooperation, effective communication, and respect for others, educators and caregivers can set a positive example for children to follow. This can include sharing decision-making responsibilities with children, listening to their ideas and concerns, and resolving conflicts in a calm and respectful manner. When children see adults working together and treating each other with kindness and respect, they are more likely to emulate these behaviors in their own interactions with their peers. By implementing strategies such as team-building activities, collaborative learning, positive reinforcement, and role modeling, educators and caregivers can help children develop important skills for successful collaboration and teamwork. These skills are not only valuable for academic success, but also for building positive relationships with others and navigating social situations throughout their lives. By investing in promoting cooperation and effective team dynamics in children, we can help them develop the necessary skills and abilities to thrive in a diverse and interconnected world.

Chapter 9: Instilling Resilience

- The importance of resilience in facing setbacks and challenges

Resilience is a crucial trait that individuals must possess in order to successfully navigate the various setbacks and challenges that life may throw their way. It is the ability to bounce back from adversity, to adapt to changing circumstances, and to persevere in the face of obstacles. In today's fast-paced and unpredictable world, resilience has become increasingly important as individuals are constantly faced with new and unexpected challenges. Whether it be a personal setback such as a job loss or a health issue, or a global crisis such as a pandemic or economic downturn, the ability to remain resilient can be a key factor in determining one's success and overall well-being.

One of the main reasons why resilience is so important is because setbacks and challenges are an inevitable part of life. No matter how well-prepared or diligent a person may be, they will inevitably encounter obstacles and setbacks along their journey. These challenges can come in many forms, whether it be personal, professional, or societal in nature. The ability to bounce back from these setbacks and effectively deal with the challenges they present is what sets resilient individuals apart from those who struggle to cope. Resilient individuals are able to maintain a positive outlook, adapt to changing circumstances, and persevere in the face of adversity, ultimately emerging stronger and more capable as a result.

In addition to helping individuals cope with setbacks and challenges, resilience also plays a crucial role in promoting mental and emotional well-being. Studies have shown that individuals who possess high levels of resilience are better able to handle stress, anxiety, and depression, and are less likely to experience negative long-term consequences as a result of difficult circumstances. This is because resilient individuals are able to effectively cope with setbacks and challenges, rather than becoming overwhelmed or defeated by them. By developing and maintaining a strong sense of resilience, individuals can protect their mental and emotional health, leading to a greater overall sense of well-being and happiness.

Furthermore, resilience is a key determinant of success in both personal and professional endeavors. In today's competitive and fast-paced world, the ability to effectively deal with setbacks and challenges can make all the difference in a person's success and achievement. Resilient individuals are able to persevere in the face of obstacles, learn from their mistakes, and adapt to changing circumstances, ultimately achieving their goals and reaching their full potential. Whether it be in a personal relationship, a career, or an academic pursuit, resilience is a key factor in determining success and realizing one's full potential.

It is important to note that resilience is not a fixed trait, but rather a skill that can be developed and strengthened over time. There are a number of strategies that individuals can use to enhance their resilience and better cope with setbacks and challenges. One such strategy is to cultivate a positive mindset and outlook, focusing on the opportunities for growth and learning that setbacks can present, rather than dwelling on the negative aspects of the situation. Additionally, practicing self-care and maintaining a healthy lifestyle can help individuals build the physical and emotional resilience needed to effectively navigate difficult circumstances. Whether it be in personal, professional, or societal contexts, the ability to bounce back from adversity, adapt to changing circumstances, and persevere in the face of obstacles is essential for achieving success and overall well-being. By developing and maintaining a strong sense of resilience, individuals can effectively cope with setbacks, protect their mental and emotional health, and ultimately achieve their goals and reach their full potential.

- Ways to help children develop a growth mindset and bounce back from failures

Developing a growth mindset is crucial for children to navigate challenges and setbacks in their academic and personal lives. A growth mindset is the belief that intelligence and abilities can be developed through effort, perseverance, and learning from failure. This mindset is in contrast to a fixed mindset, where individuals believe that their abilities are innate and cannot be improved. Research has shown that children with a growth mindset are more likely to take on challenges, persist in the face of obstacles, and ultimately achieve greater success. Therefore, it is important for parents, educators, and caregivers to support children in developing a growth mindset and bouncing back from failures.

One way to help children develop a growth mindset is to praise their efforts and strategies rather than their intelligence or talent. When children are praised for their efforts, they are more likely to see challenges as opportunities for growth and learning. On the other hand, when children are praised for their intelligence or talent, they may become overly focused on proving their abilities and avoid taking risks that could lead to failure. By praising effort and perseverance, parents and educators can reinforce the idea that success is the result of hard work and dedication.

In addition to praising efforts, it is important to teach children about the brain's ability to grow and change through practice and learning. Children should understand that the brain is like a muscle that can be strengthened through effort and practice. By learning about neuroplasticity, children can see failure as a natural part of the learning process and not as a sign of inadequacy. This understanding can help children bounce back from failures and setbacks with resilience and determination.

Another way to help children develop a growth mindset is to encourage them to set goals and work towards them with perseverance and determination. Goal-setting can help children stay motivated and focused on their personal and academic aspirations. By setting realistic and attainable goals, children can develop a sense of purpose and direction. When setbacks occur, children can use these goals as a roadmap to guide them back on track. Through goal-setting, children can learn the importance of perseverance and resilience in the face of challenges.

Furthermore, it is essential to teach children the importance of embracing challenges and stepping out of their comfort zones. By encouraging children to try new things and take risks, parents and educators can help children develop a growth mindset. When children face challenges, they have the opportunity to learn and grow from their experiences. By stepping out of their comfort zones, children can develop new skills and abilities that will serve them well in the future. Encouraging children to embrace challenges can also help them learn to bounce back from failures with grace and resilience. By praising efforts, teaching about neuroplasticity, encouraging goal-setting, and embracing challenges, parents, educators, and caregivers can support children in developing a mindset that values learning, growth, and resilience. With a growth mindset, children can navigate challenges and setbacks with confidence and determination, ultimately achieving greater success in all aspects of their lives.

Chapter 10: Cultivating Empathy

- The role of empathy in effective leadership and building relationships

Empathy is a crucial aspect of effective leadership and building relationships within any organization. It is the ability to understand and share the feelings of others, to put oneself in someone else's shoes, and see things from their perspective. This quality allows leaders to connect with their team members on a deeper level, to build trust and rapport, and to foster a sense of collaboration and understanding within the group.

In today's fast-paced world of business, where competition is fierce and pressure is high, leaders need to be able to relate to their employees in a meaningful way. By showing empathy, leaders can create a supportive and inclusive work environment where employees feel valued and appreciated. This, in turn, leads to higher levels of job satisfaction, increased productivity, and better overall performance.

Empathy also plays a key role in conflict resolution and problem-solving within an organization. When leaders can understand and acknowledge the perspectives and emotions of all parties involved in a dispute, they are better equipped to find a solution that satisfies everyone and maintains the peace. This ability to empathize with others is what sets great leaders apart from good leaders - it allows them to connect with their team members on a personal level, to inspire loyalty and commitment, and to create a positive and stimulating work environment.

Furthermore, empathy is a powerful tool for building relationships with clients, customers, and stakeholders. By putting themselves in the shoes of their customers, leaders can better understand their needs and expectations, and tailor their products or services accordingly. This not only improves customer satisfaction and loyalty but also helps to enhance the organization's reputation and brand image. In the same way, empathy can be used to build strong relationships with investors, partners, and other key stakeholders, by demonstrating an understanding of their concerns and priorities, and working collaboratively towards common goals.

It is important to note that empathy is not a sign of weakness or indecisiveness in a leader. On the contrary, it is a crucial skill that can help leaders to make better-informed decisions and to inspire and motivate their team members. By showing empathy towards others, leaders can create a positive and supportive work culture, where creativity and innovation thrive, and where individuals feel valued and respected. It allows leaders to connect with their team members on a deeper level, to understand and address their needs and concerns, and to create a positive and inclusive work environment. By cultivating empathy, leaders can foster trust, collaboration, and mutual respect within their organization, leading to increased productivity, employee satisfaction, and overall success. It is a skill that all leaders should strive to develop and nurture, as it is essential for building strong and lasting relationships, both within the organization and with external stakeholders.

- Techniques for teaching children to understand and empathize with others

Teaching children to understand and empathize with others is a crucial aspect of their overall development. Empathy is the ability to understand and share the feelings of others, and it plays a significant role in building positive relationships, fostering communication, and creating a sense of community. By teaching children empathy, we are helping them develop important social and emotional skills that will serve them well throughout their lives.

There are a variety of techniques that educators and parents can use to teach children empathy. One of the most important ways to do this is by modeling empathetic behavior. Children learn by example, so it is crucial for adults to demonstrate empathy in their own interactions with others. This can include actively listening to others, showing compassion, and acknowledging and validating others' feelings. By modeling empathy, adults can provide children with a real-life example of what it means to be empathetic.

Another important technique for teaching children empathy is to encourage perspective-taking. Perspective-taking is the ability to see things from another person's point of view, and it is a key component of empathy. One way to encourage perspective-taking is by prompting children to consider how other people might be feeling in different situations. For example, asking questions like, "How do you think your friend felt when you didn't include them in your game?" can help children begin to understand the impact of their actions on others.

In addition to modeling empathetic behavior and encouraging perspective-taking, educators and parents can also use storytelling as a tool to teach children empathy. Stories have the power to evoke emotions and help children connect with others' experiences. By reading books or watching movies that depict characters going through challenging situations, children can develop a greater understanding of different emotions and perspectives. After reading or watching a story, adults can facilitate discussions with children about the characters' feelings and motivations, helping them to empathize with the characters' experiences.

Furthermore, practicing active listening can also help children develop empathy. Active listening involves paying full attention to what someone is saying without interrupting or judging. By teaching children to listen actively to others, we are helping them develop the skills needed to understand and empathize with others' feelings. Encouraging children to ask questions, repeat back what they heard, and show empathy through their responses can help them become more empathetic individuals.

In addition to these techniques, teaching children about diversity and cultural differences can also help foster empathy. Exposing children to different cultures, religions, and traditions can help broaden their perspectives and develop a greater sense of empathy towards others who may be different from them. By teaching children to appreciate and respect the diversity around them, we are helping them develop a greater sense of empathy and understanding towards others, regardless of their background or beliefs.

It is important to note that teaching children empathy is an ongoing process that requires patience, consistency, and positive reinforcement. Children may not always understand or exhibit empathetic behavior right away, but with time and practice, they can develop the skills needed to empathize with others. By using a combination of modeling empathetic behavior, encouraging perspective-taking, storytelling, active listening, and teaching about diversity, educators and parents can help children develop the essential social and emotional skills needed to navigate their relationships and interactions with others. Ultimately, by teaching children empathy, we are helping to build a more compassionate and understanding society for future generations.

Chapter 11: Fostering Creativity

- The connection between creativity and innovative leadership

Creativity and innovative leadership are two key components in driving success and growth within organizations. Creativity is the ability to think outside the box, generate new ideas, and solve problems in unique ways. Innovative leadership, on the other hand, involves taking these creative ideas and turning them into tangible actions that drive positive change and improvement within the organization. The connection between creativity and innovative leadership lies in the fact that one cannot exist without the other. In order to be a truly innovative leader, one must be able to tap into their creative mindset and harness the power of new ideas to drive innovation and growth.

One of the key ways in which creativity and innovative leadership are connected is through the ability to inspire and motivate others. A creative leader is someone who is able to inspire their team members to think creatively, take risks, and explore new ideas. By fostering a culture of creativity and innovation within the organization, these leaders are able to motivate their team members to push boundaries and think outside the box. This in turn leads to the generation of new ideas and solutions that can drive the organization forward. Innovative leaders are also able to take these creative ideas and turn them into actionable plans that can be implemented within the organization. By being able to inspire and motivate others, creative leaders are able to leverage the power of creativity to drive innovation and success within the organization.

Another way in which creativity and innovative leadership are connected is through the ability to adapt to change and uncertainty. In today's fast-paced business environment, organizations are constantly faced with new challenges and opportunities that require innovative solutions. Creative leaders are able to thrive in these uncertain times by being able to adapt quickly to change, think creatively, and come up with new ideas and solutions. By being able to embrace change and uncertainty, these leaders are able to drive innovation and growth within the organization. Innovative leaders are also able to take these creative ideas and turn them into actionable plans that can help the organization navigate through turbulent times. By being able to adapt to change and uncertainty, creative leaders are able to leverage the power of creativity to drive innovation and success within the organization.

Furthermore, creativity and innovative leadership are connected through the ability to take risks and embrace failure. Creativity often involves taking risks and exploring new ideas that may or may not work out. Creative leaders are willing to take these risks and embrace failure as a learning opportunity rather than a setback. By encouraging their team members to take risks and explore new ideas, these leaders are able to create a culture of experimentation and innovation within the organization. This in turn leads to the generation of new ideas and solutions that can drive the organization forward. Innovative leaders are also able to take these creative ideas and turn them into actionable plans that can be implemented within the organization. By being able to take risks and embrace failure, creative leaders are able to leverage the power of creativity to drive innovation and success within the organization. Creativity is the spark that ignites new ideas and fuels innovation within organizations, while innovative leadership is the driving force that turns these creative ideas into tangible actions that drive positive change and improvement. By being able to inspire and motivate others, adapt to change and uncertainty, and take risks and embrace failure, creative leaders are able to leverage the power of creativity to drive innovation and success within the organization. Ultimately, organizations that can harness the connection between creativity and innovative leadership are better equipped to thrive in today's ever-changing business landscape.

- Activities and exercises to stimulate children's imagination and creative thinking

Children's imagination and creative thinking are vital skills that contribute to their overall development and future success. By engaging in various activities and exercises, parents and educators can help stimulate and enhance these abilities in children. There are numerous ways to encourage imaginative thinking and creativity in children, ranging from art projects and storytelling to creative play and problem-solving activities.

One effective way to stimulate children's imagination is through artistic activities such as drawing, painting, and sculpting. These activities allow children to express their thoughts and ideas visually, giving them a creative outlet for their imaginations. By providing children with a variety of art supplies and encouraging them to explore different techniques and styles, parents and teachers can help foster their artistic abilities and encourage them to think outside the box.

Another way to stimulate children's imagination is through storytelling and creative writing exercises. Children love to hear and create their own stories, allowing them to immerse themselves in imaginative worlds and characters. Parents and educators can encourage children to write their own stories, create their own characters, and even act out their stories through role-play. By engaging in storytelling activities, children can develop their narrative skills, expand their vocabulary, and enhance their creative thinking abilities.

Creative play is another important way to stimulate children's imagination and creativity. By providing children with open-ended toys and materials, such as blocks, play dough, and dress-up costumes, parents and educators can encourage children to use their imagination and creativity to create their own games and stories. Creative play allows children to explore and experiment with different ideas and concepts, helping them to develop problem-solving skills and think creatively.

Problem-solving activities can also be an effective way to stimulate children's imagination and creative thinking. By presenting children with puzzles, riddles, and brainteasers, parents and educators can encourage children to think critically and creatively to find solutions to the challenges presented to them. Problem-solving activities can help children develop their logical reasoning skills, improve their ability to think creatively, and enhance their problem-solving abilities. By engaging in artistic activities, storytelling exercises, creative play, and problem-solving activities, children can develop their imagination, creativity, and problem-solving skills. These skills are essential for children's overall development and future success, and by fostering them from a young age, parents and educators can help children reach their full potential.

Chapter 12: Promoting Goal Setting

- The significance of setting goals and working towards them in leadership development

Leadership development is a critical aspect of ensuring the success and growth of any organization. One key component of effective leadership development is the setting of goals and working towards them. Setting goals provides leaders with a clear direction and purpose, helping them to focus their efforts and energy on achieving specific outcomes. By establishing clear and measurable objectives, leaders can track their progress, identify areas for improvement, and make adjustments as needed to stay on track towards their ultimate vision.

The significance of setting goals in leadership development cannot be overstated. Goals serve as a roadmap for leaders, guiding them towards their ultimate vision and helping them to stay focused and motivated along the way. Without clear goals in place, leaders may find themselves adrift, unsure of where they are headed or how to get there. This lack of direction can lead to confusion, frustration, and ultimately, a lack of progress towards achieving organizational objectives.

In addition to providing direction and focus, setting goals in leadership development can also help to drive performance and inspire others to excel. When leaders set high, challenging goals for themselves and their teams, they create a sense of urgency and purpose that motivates individuals to push themselves beyond their comfort zones and strive for excellence. By setting ambitious goals, leaders can challenge the status quo, inspire innovation and creativity, and drive continuous improvement within their organizations.

Furthermore, working towards goals in leadership development is essential for personal growth and development. By setting goals that are aligned with their values, strengths, and aspirations, leaders can push themselves to grow, learn, and evolve as individuals. As they work towards achieving their goals, leaders will inevitably encounter obstacles, setbacks, and challenges that will test their resolve and resilience. These experiences serve as invaluable learning opportunities, helping leaders to develop new skills, overcome limitations, and become more effective and successful in their roles.

Another key benefit of setting goals and working towards them in leadership development is the ability to measure progress and track performance. By establishing clear metrics and indicators of success, leaders can monitor their progress towards achieving their goals, identify areas where they may be falling short, and take corrective action as needed to stay on track. This data-driven approach to goal-setting not only provides leaders with valuable insights into their performance but also enables them to make informed decisions and adjust their strategies and tactics as necessary to achieve their desired outcomes. By establishing clear objectives, leaders can provide themselves with direction, purpose, and focus, driving performance, inspiring others, and fostering personal growth and development. Goals not only serve as a roadmap for success but also as a catalyst for innovation, creativity, and continuous improvement within organizations. By embracing the importance of goal-setting in leadership development, individuals can unlock their full potential, achieve remarkable results, and lead their teams and organizations to new heights of success and excellence.

- Strategies for helping children identify and achieve their goals

Setting goals is an important skill for children to develop early on in life. Teaching children how to identify and achieve their goals can help them build resilience, persistence, and a sense of accomplishment. By instilling the importance of goal-setting in children, parents and educators can empower them to take control of their own futures and work towards their dreams. In this article, we will discuss strategies for helping children identify and achieve their goals.

One of the first steps in helping children identify and achieve their goals is teaching them the difference between short-term and long-term goals. Short-term goals are those that can be achieved in a relatively short amount of time, such as completing a homework assignment or learning a new skill. Long-term goals, on the other hand, are those that require more time and effort to accomplish, such as getting into a certain college or pursuing a specific career.

By helping children understand the difference between these two types of goals, parents and educators can assist them in setting realistic and achievable goals for themselves.

Another important strategy for helping children identify and achieve their goals is encouraging them to think about what they truly want to achieve. It can be easy for children to get caught up in what others want for them or what they think they should want, but it is crucial for them to identify their own passions and desires. Encouraging children to think about what truly excites and motivates them can help them set goals that are meaningful and fulfilling for them personally. By supporting children in exploring their interests and values, parents and educators can help them set goals that are in alignment with who they are and what they want to accomplish.

Once children have identified their goals, it is important to help them break them down into smaller, more manageable steps. Achieving a goal can sometimes feel overwhelming, especially if it requires a significant amount of time and effort. By breaking a goal down into smaller tasks, children can see their progress more clearly and stay motivated to continue working towards their ultimate objective. Teaching children how to create a plan of action with specific steps and deadlines can help them stay organized and focused on their goals. This strategy can also help children develop important skills such as time management and prioritization.

In addition to breaking down goals into smaller steps, it is important to encourage children to track their progress towards achieving their goals. Keeping a journal or chart to record their successes, setbacks, and the lessons they have learned along the way can help children stay motivated and accountable for their actions. By reflecting on their progress regularly, children can celebrate their achievements, learn from their mistakes, and make adjustments to their plan as needed. This practice can also help children develop a growth mindset, in which they see setbacks as opportunities for learning and growth rather than failures.

Furthermore, it is crucial for parents and educators to provide children with support and encouragement as they work towards their goals. Setting and achieving goals can be a challenging process, and children may face obstacles and setbacks along the way. By offering emotional support, praise, and guidance, parents and educators can help children stay motivated and resilient in the face of challenges. Encouraging children to ask for help when they need it and to seek out resources and mentorship can also help them overcome obstacles and stay focused on their goals. By creating a supportive and nurturing environment, parents and educators can empower children to take ownership of their goals and achieve success. By teaching children the difference between short-term and long-term goals, encouraging them to explore their passions and interests, and supporting them in breaking down their goals into manageable steps, parents and educators can empower children to set meaningful and achievable goals for themselves. By helping children track their progress, providing them with support and encouragement, and fostering a growth mindset, parents and educators can help children overcome challenges and stay motivated to work towards their dreams. By instilling the importance of goal-setting in children, parents and educators can help them develop important skills and qualities that will serve them well throughout their lives.

Chapter 13: Encouraging Adaptability

- The importance of adaptability in leadership and navigating change

In today's rapidly evolving business landscape, adaptability in leadership is becoming increasingly crucial. As organizations face constant change and disruption, leaders must possess the ability to quickly pivot and adjust their strategies to stay ahead of the curve. Adaptability is not only about being able to respond to unexpected challenges, but also about proactively seeking out opportunities for growth and innovation. In this regard, leaders who can navigate change effectively are better equipped to steer their organizations towards success in the long run.

One of the key reasons why adaptability is so important in leadership is that it enables leaders to stay agile and responsive in the face of uncertainty. In today's globalized and interconnected world, businesses are constantly exposed to a wide range of risks and opportunities. Leaders who are rigid and inflexible in their approach may find themselves unable to cope with unexpected changes or capitalize on emerging trends. On the other hand, leaders who are adaptable are able to quickly adjust their strategies and make informed decisions based on the evolving circumstances. This flexibility is essential for ensuring that organizations can not only survive, but thrive in the face of uncertainty.

In addition to being able to respond to unexpected challenges, adaptability in leadership also enables leaders to proactively seek out opportunities for growth and innovation. In a rapidly changing business environment, organizations need to be constantly looking for ways to stay ahead of the competition and drive sustainable growth. Leaders who are adaptable are able to anticipate future trends and disruptions, and can take proactive steps to position their organizations for success. By constantly questioning the status quo and being open to new ideas and perspectives, adaptable leaders can drive innovation and foster a culture of continuous improvement within their organizations.

Furthermore, adaptability in leadership is essential for building resilience within an organization. In today's volatile and uncertain world, organizations need to be able to withstand unexpected shocks and disruptions. Leaders who are adaptable are able to build flexible and agile teams that can quickly respond to changing circumstances and navigate through turbulent times. By fostering a culture of adaptability within their organizations, leaders can ensure that their teams are well-prepared to weather any storm and emerge stronger on the other side. This resilience is essential for ensuring the long-term success and sustainability of the organization.

Another important aspect of adaptability in leadership is the ability to manage change effectively. In today's fast-paced business environment, organizations are constantly undergoing various types of changes – whether it's a merger or acquisition, a reorganization, or the adoption of new technologies. Leaders who are adaptable are able to navigate these changes smoothly and effectively, ensuring that their organizations can adapt to new realities and capitalize on emerging opportunities. By being able to lead their teams through times of change, adaptable leaders can instill a sense of confidence and stability within their organizations, which can be crucial for maintaining employee morale and engagement during turbulent times. Leaders who possess the ability to navigate change and uncertainty are better equipped to drive sustainable growth, foster innovation, build resilience, and manage change effectively. By cultivating a culture of adaptability within their organizations, leaders can ensure that their teams are well-prepared to respond to the challenges and opportunities of the future. Ultimately, adaptability in leadership is not just a valuable skill – it is a prerequisite for success in today's dynamic and unpredictable world.

- Tips for helping children embrace uncertainty and learn to be flexible

In today's ever-changing world, the ability to embrace uncertainty and be flexible is a crucial skill for children to develop. As educators and parents, it is our responsibility to provide them with the tools and strategies to navigate the unknown with confidence and adaptability. By fostering a growth mindset and encouraging them to explore new opportunities, we can help children build resilience and learn to embrace uncertainty as a natural part of life.

One of the key ways to help children embrace uncertainty is to model flexibility and openness to new experiences ourselves. Children learn by example, so it is important for us to demonstrate a positive attitude towards change and uncertainty. By showing them that it is okay to make mistakes and try new things, we can encourage them to take risks and step out of their comfort zones. This can help them develop the resilience and courage to face challenges head-on and learn from their experiences.

Another important tip for helping children embrace uncertainty is to teach them the value of perseverance and problem-solving skills. When faced with a difficult or unfamiliar situation, it is important for children to learn how to break down problems into smaller, manageable steps and come up with creative solutions. By encouraging them to think critically and look for alternative approaches, we can help them develop the resilience and adaptability to overcome obstacles and navigate uncertainty with ease.

Furthermore, it is important to create a supportive and nurturing environment for children to explore and express themselves. By providing them with opportunities for creative play and self-expression, we can help children develop the confidence and self-esteem to take risks and embrace uncertainty. Encouraging them to think outside the box and explore their interests can help them develop the curiosity and adaptability to thrive in a rapidly changing world.

In addition, it is important to teach children the importance of self-care and stress management techniques to help them cope with uncertainty and build resilience. By encouraging them to engage in activities that promote relaxation and mindfulness, such as yoga, meditation, or creative expression, we can help children develop the emotional intelligence and self-awareness to navigate uncertainty with grace and poise. By teaching them how to manage their emotions and take care of themselves, we can help them build the resilience and inner strength to cope with the ups and downs of life.

Lastly, it is important to celebrate and reward children's efforts and achievements, no matter how small, to help them build confidence and self-esteem. By recognizing their progress and growth, we can help children develop a positive attitude towards change and uncertainty. By fostering a supportive and encouraging environment, we can empower children to take risks and embrace new challenges with confidence and resilience. By fostering a growth mindset, teaching problem-solving skills, and promoting self-care and stress management techniques, we can help children develop the resilience and adaptability to thrive in the face of uncertainty. By creating a supportive and nurturing environment and celebrating their efforts and achievements, we can empower children to embrace change and uncertainty with confidence and grace. It is our responsibility as educators and parents to provide them with the tools and strategies to navigate the unknown with resilience and adaptability, preparing them for a successful and fulfilling future.

Chapter 14: Nurturing Decision-Making Skills

- The role of decision-making in leadership and taking responsibility

Leadership is a complex and multifaceted concept that encompasses a wide range of skills and responsibilities. One of the key components of effective leadership is decision-making. Decision-making is the process of identifying and choosing the best course of action from among multiple alternatives. In the context of leadership, decision-making plays a crucial role in guiding the organization towards its goals and objectives.

Leaders are often faced with difficult and high-stakes decisions that have a significant impact on the organization and its stakeholders. In order to make informed and effective decisions, leaders must possess a combination of analytical, critical thinking, and problem-solving skills. They must be able to accurately assess the situation, gather relevant information, consider different perspectives, and evaluate the potential outcomes of each decision.

Taking responsibility for decisions is another important aspect of leadership. Leaders must be willing to own up to their decisions and take accountability for the consequences, both positive and negative. This involves being transparent and open about the decision-making process, communicating the rationale behind the decisions, and being willing to accept feedback and criticism. By taking responsibility for their decisions, leaders demonstrate their commitment to the organization and its values, and build trust and credibility with their team members.

Effective decision-making and taking responsibility go hand in hand in the leadership process. When leaders make well-informed decisions and take ownership of the outcomes, they demonstrate their competence and integrity as leaders. This, in turn, helps to build trust and confidence among their team members, and fosters a culture of accountability and responsibility within the organization.

In order to enhance their decision-making skills and ability to take responsibility, leaders can implement a number of strategies. One approach is to develop a systematic decision-making process that includes defining the problem, setting clear objectives, considering all available options, evaluating the potential risks and benefits, and making a final decision based on the best available information. Leaders can also seek input and feedback from their team members to gain different perspectives and insights, and to ensure that their decisions are well-informed and supported.

Another strategy for enhancing decision-making and responsibility-taking skills is to cultivate a growth mindset. This involves viewing challenges and failures as opportunities for learning and improvement, rather than as setbacks. Leaders who have a growth mindset are more likely to take risks, make tough decisions, and take responsibility for the outcomes, because they understand that failure is a normal part of the journey towards success. Leaders who possess strong decision-making skills, and who are willing to take ownership of their decisions, are better equipped to guide their organizations towards success. By developing a systematic decision-making process, seeking input and feedback from others, and cultivating a growth mindset, leaders can enhance their ability to make informed decisions and take responsibility for the outcomes. Ultimately, effective decision-making and responsibility-taking are key to building trust, credibility, and accountability within the organization, and to fostering a culture of success and growth.

- Techniques for guiding children to make informed and thoughtful choices

When it comes to guiding children to make informed and thoughtful choices, there are several techniques that can be effective in helping them develop the necessary skills and mindset. One important aspect of this process is helping children understand the consequences of their actions. By discussing potential outcomes with them, parents and educators can help children see the relationship between their choices and the results that follow. This can help children develop a sense of responsibility and accountability for their decisions.

Another technique for guiding children to make informed choices is to encourage critical thinking and problem-solving skills. By presenting children with open-ended questions and scenarios, adults can help them think through different options and consider the potential consequences of each choice. This can help children develop the ability to evaluate information, weigh different factors, and make decisions based on logic and reasoning.

In addition to encouraging critical thinking, it is important to help children develop strong communication skills. By teaching children how to express their thoughts and feelings clearly and respectfully, adults can help children articulate their needs, preferences, and concerns. This can empower children to advocate for themselves and make decisions that align with their values and priorities.

Furthermore, adults can help children develop self-awareness and emotional intelligence. By encouraging children to reflect on their thoughts and feelings, adults can help children better understand their motivations, preferences, and biases. This can help children make decisions that are aligned with their values and goals, rather than being swayed by external pressures or emotions.

It is also important to provide children with opportunities to practice making decisions in a safe and supportive environment. By allowing children to make choices and experience the consequences, adults can help children learn from their mistakes and develop confidence in their decision-making abilities. This can help children feel empowered and capable of making informed and thoughtful choices in the future. By providing children with the necessary tools and support, adults can help children develop the skills and mindset needed to navigate complex decisions and make choices that align with their values and goals.

Chapter 15: Providing Mentorship

- The benefits of mentorship in developing leadership skills

Mentorship is a powerful tool in developing leadership skills, providing guidance, support, and opportunities for growth. A mentor can offer valuable insights, advice, and feedback to help individuals navigate their career path and reach their full potential as leaders. By sharing their own experiences and knowledge, mentors can help mentees learn from both their successes and failures, accelerating their development and fostering a more confident and effective leadership style.

One of the key benefits of mentorship is the opportunity for personalized support and feedback. A mentor can provide individualized guidance tailored to the mentee's specific strengths, weaknesses, and goals, helping them identify areas for improvement and develop a strategic plan for growth. This personalized approach allows mentees to receive targeted feedback and advice that can help them overcome challenges, build on their strengths, and achieve their leadership potential.

In addition to personalized support, mentorship also offers mentees access to a broader network of resources and opportunities. Mentors can introduce mentees to new contacts, opportunities, and experiences that can help them develop their leadership skills and expand their professional horizons. By tapping into their mentor's network, mentees can gain exposure to new ideas, perspectives, and ways of thinking that can enhance their leadership abilities and deepen their understanding of the business world.

Furthermore, mentorship provides a safe space for mentees to explore new ideas, take risks, and make mistakes without fear of judgment or reprisal. A mentor can offer a supportive environment where mentees can test out new leadership strategies, experiment with different approaches, and learn from their failures in a constructive and non-threatening way. This freedom to explore and innovate can help mentees build their confidence, resilience, and adaptability as leaders, enabling them to navigate the complexities of leadership with greater skill and ease.

Another key benefit of mentorship is the opportunity for mentees to gain valuable insights and perspectives from their mentor's own experiences and expertise. Mentors can share their wisdom, lessons learned, and best practices with mentees, helping them avoid common pitfalls, learn from past mistakes, and develop a more nuanced and sophisticated understanding of leadership. By drawing on their mentor's knowledge and expertise, mentees can deepen their own leadership capabilities and gain a competitive edge in the workplace. By fostering a strong mentor-mentee relationship, individuals can accelerate their development, enhance their leadership capabilities, and achieve their full potential as leaders. To reap the benefits of mentorship, individuals should seek out mentors who are experienced, knowledgeable, and committed to their growth, and actively engage in the mentorship process by seeking feedback, exploring new ideas, and taking advantage of opportunities for growth and development. Through mentorship, individuals can leverage the wisdom, experience, and support of a mentor to unlock their leadership potential and become more effective and confident leaders in today's competitive and complex business world.

- Ways for parents to act as mentors and support their children's growth

Throughout a child's developmental journey, parental support and mentorship play a crucial role in shaping their growth and success. Parents serve as the first and most influential teachers in a child's life, providing guidance, nurturing, and encouragement every step of the way. As mentors, parents have the unique opportunity to instill values, impart knowledge, and foster important skills that will help their children navigate challenges, achieve their goals, and thrive in all aspects of life. By actively engaging in their child's growth and development, parents can create a strong foundation for their child's future success.

One of the most effective ways for parents to act as mentors and support their children's growth is through active involvement in their education. Parents can demonstrate the importance of learning by showing a genuine interest in their child's academic progress, offering help with homework, and encouraging a positive attitude towards school. By creating a supportive home environment that values education, parents can instill a strong work ethic, a thirst for knowledge, and a love of learning in their children. Additionally, parents can serve as advocates for their child's education by building relationships with teachers, attending parent-teacher conferences, and addressing any concerns or challenges that may arise.

In addition to fostering a love of learning, parents can also support their children's growth by encouraging them to explore their interests, talents, and passions. By exposing their children to a variety of activities, hobbies, and experiences, parents can help their children discover their strengths, develop new skills, and build self-confidence. Whether it's enrolling their child in extracurricular activities, encouraging them to pursue artistic or athletic endeavors, or simply exposing them to new ideas and opportunities, parents can play a key role in helping their children unlock their full potential and pursue their dreams.

Furthermore, parents can act as mentors by instilling important values and character traits in their children that will serve them well throughout their lives. By modeling good behavior, demonstrating empathy, and teaching the importance of honesty, respect, and responsibility, parents can help their children develop strong moral foundations and understand the value of integrity and ethics. By providing guidance and support in navigating ethical dilemmas, making responsible decisions, and treating others with kindness and compassion, parents can help their children become caring, principled individuals who make positive contributions to their communities and society as a whole.

Moreover, parents can support their children's growth by fostering a growth mindset and resilience in the face of challenges and setbacks. By teaching their children the value of perseverance, determination, and grit, parents can help them develop the skills and attitudes needed to overcome obstacles, learn from failures, and bounce back from disappointments. By encouraging their children to view setbacks as opportunities for growth and learning, parents can help them develop resilience, adaptability, and a positive attitude towards challenges and adversity.

Additionally, parents can act as mentors by providing emotional support, encouragement, and affirmation to their children. By listening attentively, showing empathy, and offering reassurance and comfort, parents can create a safe and nurturing environment where their children feel loved, understood, and valued. By being present, engaged, and supportive in their children's lives, parents can help them build healthy relationships, develop strong social and emotional skills, and navigate the ups and downs of adolescence with confidence and resilience. By actively engaging in their child's education, fostering a love of learning, encouraging exploration and self-discovery, instilling important values and character traits, fostering a growth mindset and resilience, and providing emotional support and encouragement, parents can create a strong foundation for their children's success in all aspects of life. Through their guidance, mentorship, and love, parents can help their children build the skills, attitudes, and values needed to thrive, achieve their goals, and make positive contributions to the world around them.

Chapter 16: Promoting Ethical Leadership

- The importance of ethical behavior and integrity in leadership

Ethical behavior and integrity are critical components of effective leadership. Leaders who demonstrate ethical behavior and uphold high standards of integrity are more likely to earn the trust and respect of their team members, colleagues, and stakeholders. This trust and respect are essential for building strong, positive relationships and fostering a culture of transparency, collaboration, and accountability within an organization.

Ethical behavior in leadership means acting with honesty, fairness, and integrity in all interactions and decision-making processes. It involves making decisions that are in the best interest of the organization and its stakeholders, even when those decisions may be difficult or unpopular. Ethical leaders prioritize the well-being of others and strive to create a work environment that is inclusive, supportive, and free from discrimination and harassment.

Integrity is closely related to ethical behavior and involves being consistent in one's actions and values, and adhering to a strong moral code. Leaders with integrity are honest, trustworthy, and dependable, and they do what they say they will do. They lead by example, demonstrating the values and principles they expect others to follow. Integrity is essential for building credibility and earning the trust of others, as people are more likely to follow leaders who consistently act with honesty and reliability.

Leaders who demonstrate ethical behavior and integrity are better able to build strong, positive relationships with their team members, colleagues, and stakeholders. When team members see their leaders acting with integrity and making ethical decisions, they are more likely to trust and respect them. This trust and respect form the foundation of a positive working relationship, where team members feel valued, supported, and empowered to do their best work. In an environment of trust and respect, team members are more likely to collaborate effectively, communicate openly, and work together towards shared goals.

Ethical behavior and integrity are also important for fostering a culture of transparency, accountability, and ethical decision-making within an organization. When leaders demonstrate ethical behavior and uphold high standards of integrity, they set a positive example for others to follow. This can help to create a culture where ethical behavior is the norm, and where team members feel empowered to speak up about unethical behavior or concerns. In a culture of transparency and accountability, unethical behavior is less likely to occur, and when it does, it is more likely to be identified and addressed promptly.

Leaders who demonstrate ethical behavior and integrity are better positioned to make sound, ethical decisions that are in the best interest of the organization and its stakeholders. By acting with honesty, fairness, and integrity, leaders can build trust and credibility with their team members, colleagues, and stakeholders. This trust and credibility are essential for effective leadership, as people are more likely to follow leaders they trust and respect. In addition, leaders who act with integrity are more likely to inspire and motivate others to do the same, creating a culture of ethical behavior and integrity within the organization. Leaders who demonstrate ethical behavior and uphold high standards of integrity are more likely to earn the trust and respect of their team members, colleagues, and stakeholders. This trust and respect form the foundation of strong, positive relationships and foster a culture of transparency, collaboration, and accountability within an organization. By acting with honesty, fairness, and integrity, leaders can create a work environment that is inclusive, supportive, and free from discrimination and harassment. Ethical leaders inspire and motivate others to do the same, creating a culture of ethical behavior and integrity that benefits the organization as a whole.

- Strategies for instilling moral values and ethical principles in children

Instilling moral values and ethical principles in children is a crucial aspect of their development that can have lasting impacts on their behavior and decision-making as they grow into adults. Parents, teachers, and caregivers play a vital role in teaching children about right and wrong, empathy, honesty, and respect for others. In this discussion, we will explore some effective strategies for instilling moral values and ethical principles in children.

One of the most important strategies for instilling moral values and ethical principles in children is to lead by example. Children learn by observing the behavior of adults around them, so it is essential for parents and caregivers to model the values and principles they want to instill in their children. This means being honest, fair, and respectful in all interactions and demonstrating empathy and kindness towards others. By consistently displaying these traits, adults can show children what it means to be a moral and ethical person.

Another effective strategy for instilling moral values and ethical principles in children is to create a supportive and nurturing environment where these values are reinforced. This can involve setting clear expectations for behavior and consistently enforcing consequences when children do not act in accordance with those expectations. It also means providing positive reinforcement when children demonstrate moral or ethical behavior, such as praising them for being honest or showing compassion towards others. By creating a supportive environment that promotes these values, children are more likely to internalize them and incorporate them into their own beliefs and actions.

In addition to modeling and reinforcing moral values and ethical principles, it is important to engage children in discussions about these topics. Encouraging children to ask questions, express their opinions, and think critically about moral and ethical issues helps them develop a deeper understanding of right and wrong. Parents and caregivers can facilitate these discussions by presenting scenarios or dilemmas for children to consider and discussing the possible outcomes and implications of different choices. By encouraging children to think about and discuss moral and ethical issues, adults can help them develop their own moral compass and ethical reasoning skills.

Teaching children about empathy is another important strategy for instilling moral values and ethical principles. Empathy is the ability to understand and share the feelings of others, and it is a key component of moral and ethical behavior. By helping children develop empathy towards others, adults can encourage them to consider the perspectives and feelings of those around them and act in a compassionate and caring manner. This can involve encouraging children to think about how their actions might impact others, teaching them to consider the feelings of others before acting, and modeling empathy in their own interactions with others.

One of the most effective ways to instill moral values and ethical principles in children is through formal education. Schools play a critical role in shaping children's beliefs and behaviors, so it is important for educators to incorporate lessons on morality and ethics into the curriculum. This can involve teaching children about the principles of honesty, integrity, fairness, and respect, as well as discussing real-world examples of moral and ethical dilemmas. By incorporating these lessons into the school day, educators can help children develop a deeper understanding of right and wrong and equip them with the knowledge and skills they need to make ethical decisions in their daily lives. By leading by example, creating a supportive environment, engaging children in discussions, teaching empathy, and incorporating lessons on morality and ethics into formal education, parents, teachers, and caregivers can help children develop a strong moral compass and ethical reasoning skills. By prioritizing the development of moral and ethical values in children, we can help them become compassionate, respectful, and responsible individuals who contribute positively to society.

Chapter 17: Embracing Diversity

- The significance of diversity and inclusion in effective leadership

Effective leadership is a crucial component of any successful organization, as it sets the tone for the entire team and ultimately determines its overall success. One key aspect of effective leadership that is often overlooked is the importance of diversity and inclusion. In today's globalized world, having a diverse and inclusive team is not just a nicety - it is a necessity. By incorporating diversity and inclusion into their leadership practices, leaders can foster innovation, creativity, and overall success within their organizations.

Diversity in leadership refers to the variety of backgrounds, experiences, and perspectives that individuals bring to a team. This can include differences in gender, race, ethnicity, age, sexual orientation, and more. Having a diverse leadership team allows for a greater range of ideas and viewpoints to be considered, leading to more creative solutions to complex problems. It also helps to avoid groupthink, where everyone in the team shares similar perspectives and fails to consider alternative viewpoints. By embracing diversity, leaders can create a more dynamic and vibrant team that is better equipped to handle the challenges of today's fast-paced and ever-changing business environment.

Inclusion in leadership, on the other hand, refers to the practice of ensuring that all team members feel valued, respected, and heard. Inclusion is about creating a sense of belonging for everyone on the team, regardless of their background or identity. When leaders foster a culture of inclusion, they create an environment where team members are comfortable sharing their thoughts and ideas, leading to greater collaboration and camaraderie within the team. Inclusive leaders encourage open communication, respect differences, and actively seek out the perspectives of all team members. By promoting inclusion, leaders can build trust and loyalty among team members, ultimately leading to higher levels of engagement and productivity.

The significance of diversity and inclusion in effective leadership cannot be overstated. Research has consistently shown that diverse teams outperform homogenous teams in terms of innovation and problem-solving. A study by McKinsey & Company found that companies with greater gender and ethnic diversity are more likely to outperform their competitors on key financial metrics. Another study by Harvard Business Review found that companies with diverse leadership teams are better able to attract top talent, improve employee satisfaction, and foster a culture of creativity and innovation. In short, diversity and inclusion are not just moral imperatives - they are also good for business.

Despite the clear benefits of diversity and inclusion, many organizations still struggle to implement effective leadership practices in this area. One common challenge is resistance to change, as some leaders may be hesitant to disrupt the status quo and embrace new ways of thinking. To overcome this resistance, leaders must be willing to challenge their own biases and assumptions, and actively seek out diverse perspectives. They can also provide training and education to help team members recognize their own unconscious biases and develop strategies for promoting inclusion.

Another challenge to effective diversity and inclusion in leadership is the lack of accountability. Without clear metrics and goals in place, it can be difficult to measure the success of diversity and inclusion initiatives. Leaders must set goals for increasing diversity within their teams, track progress towards those goals, and hold themselves accountable for achieving them. They can also implement feedback mechanisms to solicit input from team members about their experiences and ensure that everyone feels included and valued. By building diverse teams and fostering a culture of inclusion, leaders can unlock the full potential of their organizations and drive success in today's competitive business environment. Embracing diversity and inclusion is not just the right thing to do - it is also the smart thing to do. By incorporating these principles into their leadership practices, leaders can create stronger, more innovative, and more resilient teams that are better equipped to tackle the challenges of the future.

- Ways to teach children to respect and appreciate differences in others

Teaching children to respect and appreciate differences in others is a crucial aspect of their social and emotional development. In today's diverse and multicultural society, it is essential for children to learn how to embrace and celebrate the unique qualities of individuals from various backgrounds. By instilling values of tolerance, empathy, and acceptance in children from a young age, we can help create a more inclusive and harmonious community for future generations.

One effective way to teach children about respect and appreciation for differences is through education. Schools play a vital role in shaping children's attitudes and beliefs about diversity, and it is important for educators to integrate lessons on cultural awareness and inclusivity into the curriculum. By incorporating teachings on different cultures, religions, and traditions, students can gain a better understanding of the rich tapestry of human experience and learn to value the unique perspectives and contributions of each individual.

In addition to formal education, parents and caregivers also have a significant influence on children's attitudes towards diversity. By modeling inclusive behavior and promoting open-mindedness at home, adults can set a positive example for children to follow. Encouraging conversations about different cultures and fostering a sense of curiosity about the world can help children develop a more nuanced understanding of diversity and become more accepting of others who may be different from them.

Another important aspect of teaching children to respect and appreciate differences is promoting empathy and kindness. Children should be taught to treat others with compassion and understanding, regardless of their background or identity. By encouraging children to put themselves in someone else's shoes and consider how their words and actions may impact others, we can help foster a sense of empathy and emotional intelligence that is essential for building strong relationships and creating a more inclusive society.

Furthermore, promoting diversity in children's books, media, and toys can also help instill values of respect and appreciation for differences. By exposing children to a variety of perspectives and experiences through diverse representation in literature and entertainment, we can help challenge stereotypes and broaden their understanding of the world around them. Encouraging children to engage with diverse content can help expand their worldview and foster a more inclusive mindset from an early age. By incorporating lessons on diversity and inclusivity into education, modeling inclusive behavior at home, promoting empathy and kindness, and exposing children to diverse representation in media, we can help cultivate a generation of compassionate and accepting individuals who will contribute to a more harmonious and inclusive society. It is essential for adults to take an active role in shaping children's attitudes towards diversity and nurturing a culture of respect and acceptance in both the home and the classroom. Through these efforts, we can help create a more inclusive and equitable world where every individual is valued and respected for their unique qualities and contributions.

Chapter 18: Encouraging Continuous Learning

- The value of lifelong learning and personal growth in leadership development

Lifelong learning and personal growth are essential components of leadership development. In today's fast-paced and ever-changing world, leaders must continuously seek to improve and adapt in order to thrive. By committing to a lifelong journey of learning and growth, leaders can enhance their skills, expand their knowledge, and cultivate the qualities needed to effectively lead others.

One of the key benefits of lifelong learning in leadership development is the ability to stay current and relevant in an increasingly dynamic business environment. The world of business is constantly evolving, with new technologies, trends, and challenges emerging on a regular basis. Leaders who make a commitment to lifelong learning are better equipped to navigate these changes and make informed decisions that drive success. By staying informed about industry best practices, market trends, and emerging technologies, leaders can position themselves as forward-thinkers and innovators within their organizations.

Furthermore, personal growth is an essential component of effective leadership development. As leaders progress in their careers, they must also focus on their personal development in order to become more self-aware, empathetic, and resilient. Personal growth involves the cultivation of emotional intelligence, self-reflection, and the ability to adapt to change. By focusing on personal growth, leaders can enhance their communication skills, build stronger relationships with their team members, and foster a positive work environment that promotes collaboration and productivity.

Another important aspect of lifelong learning and personal growth in leadership development is the cultivation of a growth mindset. A growth mindset is characterized by a belief that abilities and intelligence can be developed through hard work, dedication, and perseverance. Leaders with a growth mindset are more likely to embrace challenges, learn from failure, and continuously seek opportunities for improvement. By cultivating a growth mindset, leaders can inspire their team members to do the same, creating a culture of learning and growth within their organizations.

In addition to staying current and fostering personal growth, lifelong learning can also help leaders develop the necessary skills and competencies to effectively lead others. Leadership is a complex and multifaceted role that requires a diverse set of skills, including decision-making, communication, problem-solving, and conflict resolution. Through lifelong learning, leaders can enhance these skills, as well as acquire new ones that are essential for success in a leadership role. By taking courses, attending workshops, and seeking out mentorship opportunities, leaders can hone their leadership skills and become more effective in guiding their teams towards success.

Furthermore, lifelong learning and personal growth can contribute to increased job satisfaction and overall well-being. As leaders continue to invest in their development, they are more likely to feel fulfilled and engaged in their work. Learning new skills and pursuing personal growth can provide a sense of accomplishment and satisfaction, leading to greater job satisfaction and a higher level of motivation. Additionally, personal growth can contribute to a sense of fulfillment and purpose in life, helping leaders to maintain a healthy work-life balance and overall well-being. By committing to a journey of continuous learning and self-improvement, leaders can stay relevant in a rapidly changing business environment, cultivate the skills and competencies needed to lead effectively, and foster a culture of growth and innovation within their organizations. Furthermore, personal growth can enhance job satisfaction, well-being, and overall success in both professional and personal life. Leaders who prioritize lifelong learning and personal growth are better equipped to navigate the complexities of leadership and inspire others to reach their full potential.

- Tips for fostering a love for learning and curiosity in children

Fostering a love for learning and curiosity in children is essential for their overall academic success and lifelong development. When children are naturally curious and eager to learn, they are more likely to be engaged in their studies and perform better in school. However, cultivating this love for learning can sometimes be challenging, especially in today's fast-paced and technology-driven world. Fortunately, there are several tips and strategies that parents and educators can utilize to help spark and nurture children's curiosity and passion for learning.

One of the most important ways to foster a love for learning in children is to create a positive and supportive learning environment. Children thrive in environments where they feel safe, respected, and encouraged to explore and ask questions. Parents and educators can create such an environment by praising children's efforts and achievements, providing constructive feedback, and promoting a growth mindset. By emphasizing the importance of effort and perseverance, children will be more likely to embrace challenges and view mistakes as opportunities for growth and learning.

Another key tip for fostering a love for learning in children is to make learning fun and engaging. Children are naturally curious and eager to explore the world around them, so it is important to harness this innate curiosity by making learning enjoyable and interactive. Parents and educators can incorporate hands-on activities, games, experiments, and real-world experiences into the learning process to help children stay engaged and motivated. By making learning fun and relevant to children's interests and experiences, they will be more likely to develop a passion for learning that will last a lifetime.

In addition to creating a positive and engaging learning environment, parents and educators can also help foster a love for learning in children by encouraging independent thinking and problem-solving skills. By giving children the freedom to explore and discover on their own, they will develop critical thinking skills, creativity, and a sense of autonomy that will serve them well throughout their lives. Encouraging children to ask questions, think critically, and find solutions to problems will help them become lifelong learners who are curious, inquisitive, and eager to learn.

Furthermore, parents and educators can foster a love for learning in children by providing them with opportunities to explore a wide range of subjects and interests. Children are naturally curious and open-minded, so it is important to expose them to a diverse range of experiences and knowledge to help them discover their passions and interests. Parents and educators can introduce children to different books, music, art, science, history, and other subjects to help them develop a broad and well-rounded knowledge base. By exposing children to a variety of topics and experiences, they will be more likely to find something that captivates their interest and sparks their curiosity.

To bring to a close, parents and educators can foster a love for learning in children by being positive role models and lifelong learners themselves. Children look up to the adults in their lives and often emulate their behavior and attitudes towards learning. By demonstrating a love for learning, curiosity, and a growth mindset, parents and educators can inspire children to follow in their footsteps and embrace learning as a lifelong journey. By showing enthusiasm for new ideas, challenges, and experiences, adults can instill a love for learning in children that will guide them through their academic careers and beyond. By creating a positive and supportive learning environment, making learning fun and engaging, encouraging independent thinking and problem-solving skills, exposing children to a wide range of subjects and interests, and being positive role models and lifelong learners themselves, parents and educators can help spark and nurture children's curiosity and passion for learning. By following these tips and strategies, adults can instill a love for learning in children that will serve them well throughout their lives and inspire them to become lifelong learners who are curious, inquisitive, and eager to explore the world around them.

Chapter 19: Emphasizing Community Engagement

- The impact of community involvement and social responsibility on leadership

Community involvement and social responsibility play a crucial role in shaping effective leadership. By actively engaging with the community and taking on social responsibilities, leaders can build trust, foster relationships, and create positive change. This not only benefits the community but also enhances the leader's reputation and credibility. In this essay, we will explore the impact of community involvement and social responsibility on leadership and discuss how it can contribute to leadership effectiveness.

One of the key ways in which community involvement and social responsibility impact leadership is through the development of strong relationships and networks. When leaders engage with the community and take on social responsibilities, they have the opportunity to connect with a diverse range of individuals and organizations. These relationships can provide valuable support, resources, and insights that can help leaders make informed decisions and navigate complex challenges. By building strong relationships with community members, leaders can also gain a deeper understanding of the needs and concerns of the people they serve, which can inform their leadership approach and priorities.

In addition to building relationships, community involvement and social responsibility can also help leaders build trust and credibility. When leaders demonstrate a genuine commitment to serving the community and taking on social responsibilities, they earn the trust and respect of those around them. This trust can be a powerful asset for leaders, as it can help them inspire and motivate others, create a sense of unity and common purpose, and overcome resistance or skepticism. By actively engaging with the community and demonstrating a willingness to address social issues, leaders can establish themselves as credible and trustworthy, which can enhance their leadership effectiveness.

Furthermore, community involvement and social responsibility can help leaders cultivate key leadership skills and qualities. When leaders engage with the community and take on social responsibilities, they have the opportunity to develop empathy, communication skills, problem-solving abilities, and cultural competency. These skills are essential for effective leadership, as they enable leaders to connect with others, understand their perspectives, and work collaboratively to address complex challenges. By actively engaging with the community and taking on social responsibilities, leaders can hone these skills and qualities, which can enhance their ability to lead with compassion, integrity, and effectiveness.

Additionally, community involvement and social responsibility can help leaders create positive change and make a meaningful impact. When leaders engage with the community and take on social responsibilities, they have the opportunity to address pressing social issues, advocate for marginalized populations, and contribute to building a more just and compassionate society. By leveraging their platform and resources to address social challenges, leaders can make a tangible difference in the lives of others and leave a lasting legacy of positive change. Through their community involvement and social responsibility efforts, leaders can inspire others to take action, build momentum for social change, and create a more inclusive and equitable society. By actively engaging with the community, building strong relationships, earning trust and credibility, cultivating key leadership skills and qualities, and creating positive change, leaders can strengthen their leadership capabilities and make a meaningful impact on their communities. It is clear that community involvement and social responsibility are essential components of effective leadership, and leaders who prioritize these aspects are better equipped to inspire, motivate, and lead with compassion, integrity, and effectiveness. As such, it is important for leaders to embrace community involvement and social responsibility as integral parts of their leadership approach in order to maximize their impact and create positive change in the world.

- Activities and projects to engage children in giving back and making a difference

Engaging children in giving back and making a difference is a crucial aspect of their development as well-rounded individuals. Teaching children the importance of empathy, compassion, and social responsibility from a young age can have a lasting impact on their values and behavior as they grow older. There are various activities and projects that can be implemented to help children understand the concept of giving back and making a positive impact in their communities.

One effective way to engage children in giving back is through volunteering opportunities. Volunteering not only allows children to contribute to a cause they are passionate about, but also helps them develop a sense of empathy and understanding of those less fortunate than themselves. There are many volunteer opportunities that are suitable for children, such as helping out at a local soup kitchen, organizing a donation drive for a homeless shelter, or participating in a community clean-up project. By participating in these activities, children can learn the importance of giving back and making a difference in the lives of others.

Another way to engage children in giving back is through fundraising events. Fundraising events can be a fun and interactive way for children to raise awareness and support for a cause they care about. Children can organize events such as bake sales, car washes, or charity walks to raise money for a local charity or organization. By participating in fundraising events, children can learn important skills such as event planning, marketing, and teamwork, while also making a positive impact in their community.

In addition to volunteering and fundraising, engaging children in hands-on projects can also help them understand the importance of giving back. One example of a hands-on project is creating care packages for those in need. Children can gather items such as toiletries, non-perishable food, and clothing, and assemble care packages to donate to a local shelter or charity. This project not only teaches children the importance of helping others, but also allows them to see the direct impact of their actions on those in need.

Furthermore, involving children in environmental projects can also help them understand the importance of giving back to the planet. Children can participate in activities such as planting trees, cleaning up litter in their community, or starting a recycling program at their school. By engaging in these environmental projects, children can develop a sense of responsibility towards the environment, and learn the importance of taking care of the world around them. By teaching children the importance of empathy, compassion, and social responsibility, we can help them become responsible and caring individuals who are committed to making a positive impact in the world. Through volunteering, fundraising, hands-on projects, and environmental initiatives, children can learn valuable lessons about the power of giving back and the difference they can make in their communities.

Chapter 20: Conclusion

- Recap of key concepts and strategies for raising a successful, future leader

Leadership is a key aspect of any organization, whether it be a business, non-profit, or government agency. Effective leadership is crucial for the success and sustainability of an organization, as leaders are responsible for guiding and motivating their teams, making crucial decisions, and setting the overall direction of the organization. In today's rapidly changing and complex business environment, it is more important than ever for organizations to develop and nurture future leaders who have the skills, knowledge, and mindset necessary to navigate these challenges.

One of the key concepts in raising a successful future leader is the importance of developing strong emotional intelligence. Emotional intelligence refers to the ability to understand and manage one's emotions, as well as the emotions of others. Leaders with high emotional intelligence are better able to build strong relationships with their teams, navigate conflicts, and make informed decisions. To develop emotional intelligence in future leaders, organizations can provide training and coaching in areas such as self-awareness, self-regulation, empathy, and social skills.

Another key concept for raising successful future leaders is the importance of fostering a growth mindset. A growth mindset is the belief that one's abilities and intelligence can be developed through hard work, effort, and persistence. Leaders with a growth mindset are more likely to embrace challenges, learn from failure, and continuously seek to improve themselves and their teams. To foster a growth mindset in future leaders, organizations can create a culture that values learning and innovation, provides opportunities for professional development and feedback, and encourages a mentality of continuous improvement.

In addition to emotional intelligence and a growth mindset, another important concept for raising successful future leaders is the ability to think strategically. Strategic thinking involves the ability to see the big picture, anticipate future trends and challenges, and develop innovative solutions to address them. Future leaders who can think strategically are better equipped to make sound decisions, set ambitious goals, and lead their organizations to success. To develop strategic thinking in future leaders, organizations can provide training in areas such as problem-solving, decision-making, scenario planning, and strategic planning.

Furthermore, effective communication is another key concept for raising successful future leaders. Communication skills are essential for leaders to convey their vision, goals, and expectations to their teams, as well as to build trust, inspire motivation, and resolve conflicts. Future leaders who can communicate effectively are more likely to build strong relationships with their teams, influence others, and drive positive change within their organizations. To develop effective communication skills in future leaders, organizations can provide training in areas such as public speaking, active listening, conflict resolution, and feedback giving.

Lastly, cultivating resilience is a crucial concept for raising successful future leaders. Resilience refers to the ability to bounce back from setbacks, adapt to change, and persevere in the face of adversity. Future leaders who are resilient are better able to navigate challenges, learn from failure, and lead their teams through difficult times. To cultivate resilience in future leaders, organizations can provide opportunities for them to take risks, learn from failure, and develop coping strategies for stress and uncertainty. By developing emotional intelligence, a growth mindset, strategic thinking, effective communication, and resilience in future leaders, organizations can help ensure that they are well-equipped to lead their organizations to success in an increasingly complex and uncertain business environment.

- Final thoughts on the importance of parental guidance and support in nurturing tomorrow's leaders.

Parental guidance and support play a crucial role in molding and nurturing the future leaders of tomorrow. As children grow and develop, they are greatly influenced by the environment in which they are raised, and parents are often their primary role models and sources of guidance. It is important for parents to instill good values, morals, and ethics in their children from a young age, as these qualities are essential for effective leadership in the future.

One of the key ways in which parental guidance and support shape future leaders is through the development of important life skills. From communication and problem-solving to decision-making and conflict resolution, these skills are essential for effective leadership. Parents can help their children develop these skills by providing opportunities for them to practice and refine them, as well as by modeling them in their own behavior. By instilling these skills in their children, parents are helping to prepare them for the challenges and responsibilities of leadership in the future.

In addition to fostering important life skills, parental guidance and support also play a crucial role in shaping the values and beliefs of future leaders. Parents have the opportunity to teach their children about the importance of integrity, honesty, and compassion, and to instill in them a sense of social responsibility and a commitment to making a positive impact on the world. By imparting these values to their children, parents are helping to ensure that they will become leaders who are guided by a strong moral compass and who are committed to making ethical decisions that benefit the greater good.

Furthermore, parental guidance and support are essential for fostering a sense of self-confidence and self-esteem in future leaders. Children who are raised in a supportive and nurturing environment are more likely to develop a strong sense of self-worth and self-belief, which are essential for effective leadership. By providing their children with encouragement, praise, and constructive feedback, parents can help them develop the confidence and resilience they need to navigate the challenges and setbacks that come with leadership roles. Additionally, parents can help their children identify and build on their strengths, talents, and interests, which can further boost their self-esteem and sense of purpose.

Moreover, parental guidance and support are instrumental in helping future leaders develop strong emotional intelligence and interpersonal skills. Emotional intelligence, which encompasses self-awareness, self-regulation, empathy, and social skills, is a critical component of effective leadership. Parents can help their children develop these skills by teaching them to recognize and manage their emotions, to empathize with others, and to communicate effectively. By fostering emotional intelligence in their children, parents are helping to prepare them for the complex interpersonal dynamics and relationships that are inherent in leadership roles. By instilling important life skills, values, self-confidence, emotional intelligence, and interpersonal skills in their children, parents are laying the foundation for them to become effective and ethical leaders in the future. It is crucial for parents to be actively involved in their children's upbringing, to serve as positive role models, and to provide them with the love, guidance, and support they need to reach their full potential as leaders. By investing in their children's development and well-being, parents are not only shaping the future of their children but also the future of society as a whole. Ultimately, the importance of parental guidance and support in nurturing tomorrow's leaders cannot be overstated, as it is through the guidance and support of parents that the leaders of tomorrow will be prepared to meet the challenges and opportunities that lie ahead.